ARABIC PROSE COMPOSITION

ARABIC PROSE COMPOSITION

by

T. H. WEIR, B.D., M.R.A.S.

Lecturer in Arabic in the University of Glasgow.

Cambridge :
at the University Press
1910

CAMBRIDGE
UNIVERSITY PRESS

University Printing House, Cambridge CB2 8BS, United Kingdom

Cambridge University Press is part of the University of Cambridge.

It furthers the University's mission by disseminating knowledge in the pursuit of
education, learning and research at the highest international levels of excellence.

www.cambridge.org
Information on this title: www.cambridge.org/9781316626085

First published 1910
First paperback edition 2016

A catalogue record for this publication is available from the British Library

ISBN 978-1-316-62608-5 Paperback

TO

PAST AND PRESENT
STUDENTS OF ARABIC

IN

THE UNIVERSITY OF GLASGOW

CONTENTS

PREFACE

THE exercises contained in the following pages are intended to carry the student of Arabic on from the rudiments of the Language to what may be considered advanced prose.

The Preliminary Exercises (Part I) are to be used during the study of the grammar and syntax. References have been added at the foot of the page to the late Mr Thornton's useful abridgement of Wright's *Arabic Grammar* edited by Mr R. A. Nicholson, M.A., for the Cambridge University Press; but as the ground covered in each exercise is indicated in the heading, the student may use any grammar to which he is accustomed. Indeed, a progressive grammar of Classical Arabic, on the principle of the late Professor Davidson's *Elementary Hebrew Grammar*, is still a *desideratum*.

The Proses in Part II have been selected for the most part from Vols. I and II of the admirable *Majāni'l-Adab* published by the Jesuit Fathers in Beyrout, but also from other sources; and those in Part III from the weekly edition of the famous Cairo newspaper *Al-Muaiyad*, edited by the Sheikh Ali Yusuf; whilst those in Part IV consist of extracts from the *Times*, from Lord Cromer's *Modern Egypt*, and other sources, which were reproduced in an Arabic version in the columns of the *Muaiyad*. To each of the first sixteen of these there has been added a "literal version," which should be carefully compared with the original and then translated into Arabic. In the case of the remainder, as in the earlier parts, footnotes have been considered sufficient.

There is nothing incongruous in attempting to combine in one volume the classical and the modern Arabic. Every Egyptian newspaper reflects in some measure the language of the Koran and of the ancient poets, just as an English journal does that of the Bible and of Shakespear, and the reader who is not familiar with these misses much of the pith and marrow of the composition. Moreover, whatever may be said of some products of the Syrian and Egyptian press, the *Muaiyad* is distinguished for the excellent Arabic in which its articles are composed.

In Parts I, II and III of the present work any considerations of style have been sacrificed to the desire to make the English reflect the required Arabic expression as closely as possible. In this way the student will become more familiar with the Arabic idiom, and it will be a good exercise for him to turn this Arabic-English into King's English. As a general rule it may be said that the most difficult passage can be most easily rendered into Arabic by first of all re-writing it in the simple Saxon-English of the Bible, particularly of the Old Testament.

In the glossary the vowel-points have been omitted in cases where they can easily be supplied, and, generally, it has been left to the student to make forms for himself, rather than that they should be given him ready made. If a word is not given in the glossary, it is for this reason, or because it is not required. It is necessary to warn the beginner that the Arabic words given in the glossary are the equivalents of the English only in the particular sense in which the latter happen to occur in the text.

My best thanks are due to the Rev. Professor James Robertson, D.D., LL.D. and to Mr Alexander S. Fulton for their kindness in reading the proof-sheets of the whole book: to the Messrs Macmillan for their permission to reprint the passages from Lord Cromer's *Modern Egypt*; and to the readers and compositors of the Cambridge University Press for the extreme care and accuracy with which the work of printing has been done.

T. H. WEIR.

GLASGOW UNIVERSITY, 1910.

PART I

PRELIMINARY EXERCISES

TRANSLITERATION

Consonants.

ا	= '	ط	= ṭ
ب	= b	ظ	= ẓ
ت	= t	ع	= '
ث	= th	غ	= gh
ج	= j	ف	= f
ح	= ḥ	ق	= q
خ	= kh	ك	= k
د	= d	ل	= l
ذ	= dh	م	= m
ر	= r	ن	= n
ز	= z	ه	= h
س	= s	و	= w
ش	= sh	ى	= y
ص	= ṣ	ة	= ħ
ض	= ḍ		

Vowels and Diphthongs.

ـَ = a	اـً = an	ٲ = ā			
ـِ = i	ـٍ = in	ـِى = ī			
ـُ = u	ـٌ = un	ـُو = ū			
	ـًى = ai		ـًو = au		

1. ORTHOGRAPHY.

Transliterate :

a. (Consonants¹). bt dr rs sr ḍd ṭḥ 'f d' qd fq lm ml fk kn hw ny byn ywm dyn rqṣ rkḍ dlw klb qlq 'rḍ nẓm nzl hyj bṭn tbn mrw bdl llh msjd ḫjj krsy b'yr ṭybh d̲h̲bḥ k̲h̲lyfḥ s̲h̲ms t̲h̲bt g̲h̲rḍ s̲h̲g̲h̲l ṣḥyḥ mkḥ bhm k̲h̲ṭb tm swrḥ lylḥ b's s'l 'k̲h̲dh l'd̲h̲bnk.

b. (Vowel-signs²). bā lī fū hal lima kul sir qad haraba qutila yanzilu rajul*un* rajul*in* rajul*an* qaryat*an* madīnat*un* madīnat*in* madīnat*an* kūtiba yukātibu hud*an* zakātu ṣalātu ḥayātu ramā dunyā yaḥyā taurātu kalamū yaklimū.

c. (Hamzaḥ³). 'asad*un* 'ibil*un* 'umira sa'ala su'ila su'āla ka'iba baṭu'a qara'a yaqra'u fati'a yafta'u yabda' mil'*un* ẓim'*an* yabū'u bā'a yajī'u yusī'ūna 'abnā'u 'abnā'uhu 'abnā'a 'abnā'ahu 'abnā'i 'abnā'ihi ru'ūsu tajī'ūna.

d. (Tas̲h̲dīd⁴). kallama kallim takallumu saiyidu hauwana khuyyila ḥimār*un* ḥammār*un* dābbatī duwaibbatī fārra fūrira 'ak̲h̲k̲h̲arat maiyit*un*.

Prefix the Definite Article to the following :

Qamaru 'insānu baitu jāru khālu 'ainu ghaibu mar'u hawānu Shamsu thauru dalwu ra'su sairu naumu mautu ẓannu waladu yadu 'ahlu lailu 'ilāhu.

Transliterate :

e. (Maddaḥ⁵). mālu 'ālu 'akala 'ākala ya'kul 'ākul yu'kal 'ūkal yu'min 'ūmin mu'minu kātibu 'ākilu 'iqtālu 'īmānu qāla jā'a sāra s̲h̲ā'a sakrānu mal'ānu.

f. (Waṣlaḥ⁶). Prefix (1) the Article (2) qāla (3) qālat (4) hum (5) ra'au (6) 'au (7) min (8) tarai (9) rajul*un* to the Arabic words for name, son, two.

---

¹ Du Pre Thornton's *Elementary Arabic*, §§ 1, 2.
² Thornton, §§ 4–10.   ³ Thornton, §§ 15–17.
⁴ Thornton, §§ 11, 14.   ⁵ Thornton, §§ 22, 23, 132.
⁶ Thornton, §§ 18–21.

Write in Arabic the following pairs of words:

Qāla uḵẖruj : qālat idẖḥab : qālū ijlis : rajul*un* ismuhu : min ismihi : min al-ismi : kataba al-isma : qatala al-ibna : min al-ibni : naẓara iṯẖnaini : lāqau iṯẖnaini : min al-iṯẖnaini : ḍarabū al-rajula.

g. Write the Arabic for:

a. (With the vowel-signs):

Adam, Jerusalem, Job, Babylon, Umaiyah, Ishmael, Othman, Mohammad, Lokman, Thamud, Idris, Omar, Barzakh, Ramadan, Honein, Mecca, denier, Midian, Medina, Yathrib, Shoaib, the Gospel, Sinai, Noah, Goliath, Kisra, the Greeks, the Christians, the Jews, Gog, Magog, India, Iblis, the Satan, Irem, Pharaoh, Egypt, the Safa, the Merwah, Gabriel, Michael, Coreish, Moses son of Amram, Jesus son of Mary, Solomon son of David, Joseph son of Jacob son of Isaac son of Abraham, Buzurjumihr, Anusharwan.

β. (Without the vowel-signs):

Victoria, England, London, France, Paris, Germany, Russia, Siberia, Manchuria, the Hungarians, Austria, Italy, Europe, Duchess, Turkey, firman, the *Times*, Britain, British, Sardinia, the Vatican, Catholic, Pope, Mr, Monsieur, Bombay, boulevards, Port Arthur, Khedive, centimetre, kilometre, pasha, police, Jeved, Bosnia, Herzegovina, Haicheng, Ascalon, October, November, December, philosopher, Euclid, Aristotle, Macedonia, Pharisee, locomotive, franc, the Franks.

2. FORMS OF THE VERB[1].

It was much. He made much. He desired much. He knew. He taught. He learned. He slew. He massacred. He fought. There fought mutually. He gave pardon. He asked pardon. He declared true. He declared false. He was truthful. He lied. He healed. He blessed. He became blessed. He turned aside (intr.). He exchanged. He gave in exchange.

[1] Thornton, §§ 35–68.

4

He took in exchange. He furnished. He was good. He did good.
He veiled himself. He mixed. It mixed with (tr.). It mixed
(intr.). He was in a hurry. He hurried. He asked to be
hurried. He declared unlawful. He warred. There warred
mutually. He disputed with. He stored up for himself. He
contradicted. There disagreed. He sacrificed. He slaughtered.
He spoke. There spoke to one another. He committed crime.
It turned black. It became black. He divided. He objurgated.
He waged holy war. He recollected himself. He thought weak.
He excused himself. He turned round. It became white. He
managed. He turned his back. He planned. It (star) went
up. He surveyed. He shouted. He smiled. He followed.
He accompanied. He carried. He loaded. He was hump-
backed. He strove with. There strove. It quaked. He made
to quake. He philosophized. He was comfortable. He lay on
his face. He stretched his neck.

3. THE STRONG VERB[1] (INCLUDING PARTICIPLES AND INFINITIVES).

You went out. You will go out. Go out! He will push.
Push! They will be niggardly. They were niggardly. They
lost. Let them indeed take oath. You assailed. We fretted.
The two rode. Ride! He was chid. They were asked to
preserve. Be firm. Make firm. Go away you two. I will
indeed punish. Spy out. They will be defrauded. He was
dislodged. You made a treaty with. You reaped. Dissipating.
Cowering. The rightly guided. You were in grievous case.
Let him beware. It will bristle. They came on the scene. You
are ignorant. She shrivelled. Turn away! She will tell news.
It is destined. He was blessed. Blessed. He will be incar-
cerated. You will be enchanted. Make public. We perverted.
She was heavy. It was likened. Lash! They understand.
They were noticed. You disputed. Sent. They will suckle.
He was loaded. Frozen. I was keen-sighted. Let them be

[1] Thornton, §§ 73–117, 196, 202, 230, 236.

keen-sighted. Having shaved. Leave alone! Wait! Vain.
Send! Those in despair. They will belie. Lowly. They are
expecting. It was ransacked. He will be crucified. She was
brought nigh. Disliked. He will indeed help. They were convulsed.
Convulsion. The spendthrifts. You will wear. You will
confuse. She will be comfortable. You stretched out. Anni-
hilating. It was rolled. She was troubled. She was made to
quake. Holy war. To teach. Teacher. Juggler. They will
encamp.

4. DOUBLED VERBS[1].

Shake! They will keep on. I perfected. He perfected.
He will perfect. Perfect! Love! I was returned. Let him
dictate. He will indeed touch. He will verify. They persisted.
You were forced. I erred. You will indeed stretch out. They
will obstruct. That we may be abased. You abase. Let him
indeed debar. She hides. He will pull. Blamed. She will
gladden. They kept secret. It harms. Restrain. She was
plucked up. He will thrust. They will be thrust. They will
fall down. It is lawful. A pilgrim. Dispersed. He will
swoop. They will argue with. They will argue with one
another. We split. Pour! We will recount. Setting free.
You slipped. Let them revile. He will bind firmly. Bind
firmly. Dismiss! You will flee. That you may be pious. Let
him abstain. Let them abstain. Threaten!

5. VERBS WITH HAMZAH[2].

Ask! Asked. He was asked. It will be asked. He ran
away. It was founded. You prefer. We have missed. They will
turn away in disgust. Brought together. You will indeed announce.
He declared innocent. I will command. You have hired. I will

[1] Thornton, §§ 120–124.
[2] Thornton, §§ 130–140.

indeed fill. She was filled. You have been assigned a date.
Censured. Believe! They believed. We shall believe. Belief.
A believer. Take! Take to yourselves! You will thirst. Let
them ask to be allowed. They will repel. You repelled one
another. They will be changed in nature. He will begin. He
will indeed delay much. Eat. Command. And command.
And eat. Eating. You find out. That they may extinguish.
A congress. Then allow! O Musa, allow!

6. Verbs first radical weak[1].

He will find. Let him find. She was afraid. May you be
afraid. Let. He slumbered. He will slumber. Slumber. To
slumber. He will place. They will place. It was placed. It
will be kindled. They describe. You promised. You were
promised. You will be promised. He was menaced. You will
be menaced. He will arrive. That it be joined. He was made
agent. Rely! May she bear. He will be born. Give! We
will brand. You will indeed forsake. They shall be certain.
He will inherit. We made to inherit. I will exhort. Exhort!
He will be exhorted. We made easy. They will tread. Buried
alive. He will whisper. They were stood (made to stand). It
occurred. I will awake.

7. Verbs second radical weak[2].

We drove. We will drive. It will be rained on. You died.
You put to death. They will pass the night. They will meditate
by night. They gave by measure. They took by measure. I
repented. They repented. He will repent. Repent! Take
provisions. They took provisions. You waded. We will wade.
We will fear. The being within reach of one another. It will
be fancied. We ornamented. They were traitors. She tasted.

[1] Thornton, §§ 142–148, etc.
[2] Thornton, §§ 149–157, etc.

Taste! Tasting. We will indeed make to taste. He bestowed. It was intervened. He was disappointed. He increased. He was debating with. You visited. Let us become masters. She was married. They were made to return. They will receive protection. He demanded protection. Give protection. You will be able. I sought refuge. Say, I seek refuge in God. The two passed on. They were sceptical. Sceptic. Causing doubt. Let him deviate. Obey! Obeying. Obeyed. The two came to naught. That they come to naught. It will be circumambulated. We flooded. Hunt! I will plot a plotting. I am almost. I will make to perish. Said a sayer. She has embellished.

8. Verbs third radical weak[1].

They met. Cast! They cast. It flows. That he may reward. It was empty. They were empty. Let him be empty. I am satisfied. I dreaded. They will dread. Let him dread. Dread! Hope! Hoped. You are satisfied. They will satisfy. They were guided. Guide! Let him throw. Travel by night! I recited. I will recite. Recite! It will be recited. He is insolent. Go out in the morning. They were called to. We have proved. He selected. Drawing near. Herd! The two are on a level. They conspire. We will indeed deliver. You will weep. You will conceal. She will be concealed. He will purify himself. I complain. He will remain. Remaining. It will earn interest. Named. They two will want. Wanting for oneself. We shall be put to shame. You claim. They were miserable. Past. Walk! She was visible. They will make visible. They will be adorned. It revealed itself. They will quarrel. She will contemn. He transgresses. Elect. They bought. Forgive! May it be forgiven[2]. He will cover. He will be covered. They made fun. They prohibited. They will prohibit. They were prohibited. I was prohibited. He amended. They will ask for a decision. May you track.

---

[1] Thornton, §§ 164–170, etc.   [2] pf.

9. Verbs doubly and trebly weak, defective, etc.[1]

We granted a revelation. Let a revelation be granted. I would. May you guard. Reverence! The reverencing. You will indeed see. She saw. Do you see? We showed. I will show. They will be shown. She was paid in full. She will be paid in full. They came back. You will come back. You will cause to come back. Take up your quarters. Folded. They [Moslems] will die. She was evil. It will be evil. She was displeased. They made evil. He lit up. He will light up. I will indeed mislead. Fit out! It will cover over. It was covered over. That I may cover over. They will molest. They despaired. Let them despair. I came. They came. Come. Then come. He said, Come. Say, Come. She was brought. We shall be brought. Coming. Bringing. Pay! Let her grieve. Good! Ill it is! He will live. Wish long life! He made live. He will make live. He will be ashamed. They will let live. Modesty. I will lodge myself. They lodged Moses. Let him refuse. They will. He willed. Let him will. Good is the educator, Fortune[2]!

10. The Verbal Suffixes[3].

We annihilated them. It will indeed seduce you. We drowned them. You will imprison the two of them. You disliked them. We let him enjoy. She will instigate them. It aided it. They will be responsible for him. It diverted you. Deliver us. Guard them. They feel a desire for it. He forged it. We came to them. They were brought it. Hire him! Take him! He will put them off (postpone). Let him pay it.

---

[1] Thornton, §§ 171–183, etc.   [2] the times.
[3] Thornton, §§ 185–189.

We notified you. I see me. We ransomed him. He will ransom himself. We cast a spell on her. It covers it. You (women) blamed me. We strengthened him. I chose you. Take yourselves off from me. We created them both. You made me successor. You put him to shame. We numbered them. We revealed her. Thee we will kill and him we will let live. They introduced it. He anchored her. We rewarded them. You envy us. We will put him to the proof. Beware of them. He will bid you beware of them. He will congregate them. It has reached me. They will be present with me. We will indeed present them. He will ask you for it. We will lead them on by degrees. He built it. He rewarded them. Glorify Him. You noticed them. We sent them. He will bring you good tidings. He will fashion you. They will anticipate us. We will necessitate it to you. He will suffice you against them. We showed you them. He will show you them. I will marry her to you. He married her to him. Give it me. I give it you. Thee we will beat. They beat us and them.

11. The Pronouns[1].

Who (are) you? I (am) Musa. What (is) this? It (is) a house. Who (is) she? This (is) Hind. Where (are) they? They (are) here. What (are) these? These (are) the Greeks. Who (are) those? Those (are) Christians. Who (are) these two? Those two (are) Moses and Solomon. Who did this? He killed them (two). Who beat you (two)? He beat us. What did they (do)? They slaughtered it. This (is) Joseph who killed Moses. Those are the Jews whom we killed. He slaughtered the (two) whom they beat. Remember me. He will forget us. How many an opportunity[2] has gone away!

---

[1] Thornton, §§ 89, 185–189, 317, etc.   [2] gen.

12. DECLENSION OF NOUNS AND ADJECTIVES, CONSTRUCT STATE, SUFFIXES[1].

A dwelling. A city. Of a dwelling. Of a city. He built a dwelling. He founded a city. This is a house. That is a city. An open[2] letter. A large house. A small city. These are folk. The wrong-doing folk. The political horizon. This is larger than that. The largest house. The largest city. Of a black thread. Of the black thread. A yellow camel. A yellow cow. Another day. Another night. A black (man). A black (woman). A thirsty camel. A thirsty cow. This is the son of the king. The king's large house. The dwelling of the great king. Another verse. Other folk. The most of them. Many fruits. Two consecutive months. These two gardens. The two men. The first[3] of them. The other[3] of them. One of them. His hand is white. My book. His house. Our city. Of their dwelling. Which of them is best? The going up and setting of the sun. The house and garden of the king. He is dumb, deaf, blind. A blind woman. The best of the affairs is the mean of them. The head of the wisdom is the fear of God. The King and Queen of England. (The) science ornaments the kings more than (what) it ornaments the subjects. The very hot water (the water the violent of the hotness). The present state of things.

13. THE BROKEN PLURALS, NUMERALS, PARTICLES[4].

A large book. Large books. Many days. Reckoned days. Other days. In this city is much folk. Different colours. Their works are sound. We journeyed thirty nights. There will be overtaken the needs. I saw four men. There disagree the learned. They sought his traces. The sound sheikhs. The

[1] Thornton, §§ 234, 308–317, 475–493.   [2] opened.   [3] fem.
[4] Thornton, §§ 304–307, 318–328, 354–368, 496–506.

good quality of the eatables. This is better for you. To it are
advantages. Our houses. His verses. Aims. Weights. The
present interests. Old tombs. Mighty sultans. Apostles.
Four weeks. Three years. Ten bushels. Great treasures. In
that land are many tanks. White swords. Many telegrams.
There fought the Syrians the Turks. These are strange tales.
In the library are journals and magazines. The legal sciences.
This is a French steamship. The farmers. Articles. His horses.
He was of the Sufis. In the book are figures. His features are
refined. Twelve women. Two and two (are) four. Men are
three, the intelligent, the stupid, and the wicked. These are the
king's yachts. Wisps of dreams.

14. The Tenses[1].

He beats. He is beating. He used to beat. He beat. He
has beaten. He had beaten. He will have beaten. Seek one
who will dine with us. They sought, then did not find. Thy
brother is he who speaks thee true. At the being tested the
man will be honoured or despised. He erred whom the blind
were guiding. How should (the) history be taught? By Allah,
I never stole anything in my life[2]. They did not cease talking to
him with the roughest of the talk. Al-Hasan was not seeing
good the fighting, but was wishing that he should take to
himself[3] what he was able from Muawiya. Let there not (indeed)
seduce thee the ascent, even if it were plain when the descent
was rugged. I ask you that you forgive him. They used to
dislike that there should be in the khalifs and kings acuteness
and knowledge of (the) affairs. When the month of Ramadan
came in[4] there were placed before[5] him (the) books of history
and biographies and the scribe[6] and the recorder would read

[1] Thornton, §§ 401–409.
[2] I did not steal my lifetime a thing.   [3] his soul.   [4] entered.
[5] presented to.   [6] writer.

before him[1] the states of the world. I do not know which (of the two) is the more wonderful. In this month the Nile will have started the decrease. May God have mercy upon him.

15. THE MOODS[2].

I will kill both of them, or else die instead of them. Do good if you wish that good should be done unto you. The worst of men is he who does not care that men see him. Do not prohibit from a character and come[3] to the like of it. He who does not honour[4] himself (his soul) will not be honoured[4]. Look how his subjects assembled against him from every side. I will come to you to-morrow. In that case I will honour you. The slave will not be loving (to) his Creator until he lavish his soul in His satisfaction. Do not say in other than considering, and do not work by other than management. Am I able after that that I should imagine that you are an honourable man ? The most of men feel a desire that they should be rich, and seek the much money. If anyone makes the kindness in other than his own people, his praise upon him shall be[4] blame and he shall feel remorse[4]. I will not (it will not be that I shall) leave Egypt. One of the wise looked at (unto) a fool sitting upon a stone: then he said, Stone upon stone. He fainted and almost died, then he recovered.

16. THE ACCUSATIVE[5].

They (two) fell slain. I tarried by his side an hour. There is no first to His existence and no last to his everlastingness ; and there is not any motion and quiescence except and to Him in that is wisdom. Know that the Creator—exalted be He— there is not to Him a figure. This world is like the salt water : in proportion as the companion of it increases in drinking he

---

[1] between his hands.   [2] Thornton, §§ 411–420.   [3] subjunctive.
[4] apoc.   [5] Thornton, §§ 421–444.

increases in thirsting; and like the lightning which lights up for
a little and goes away speedily and the hoper of it remains in the
darkness staying. He had attained in seclusion from this world
a mighty attainment. He staid in that state[1] (some) days. O
you there, do you boast yourself in an affair you will leave (alone)
to-morrow? There is no apostle like the dirhem. There is no
money more copious than (the) intellect, and there is no poverty
mightier than (the) ignorance. I wonder (with) all of the wonder
at what he has done. This study shall be optional. If the breast
of the man be too narrow for his own secret[2], then the breast
of him with whom the secret is deposited (is) narrower. The
English have taken in hand every administration in this country
except the administration of the Azhar and that of the endow-
ments, for they (two) continue native. I will dispose of Muawiya
for you[3]. Verily I and they are like one going down to (a goer
down of) a watering place. You have no father.

17. Prepositions and Similar Words[4].

It does not require proof. And is the flesh capable of[5] the
like of this? Preserve carefully (upon) the friend, even if (he
were) in Hell. Many a weariness leads to rest. Perhaps was
the silence an answer. The most difficult of what is (incumbent)
upon man is the knowledge of himself. The putting of the doing
good in other than its place is wronging. The sound opinion is
more protecting than the violent hero. Every science which is
not in (the) paper is lost[6]; every secret which passes on (beyond)
the two (people) spreads[6]. There was to me a friend whom I
loved for his excellence and his education more than (what) I
loved him for his soundness and religion. After the storm.
Approach one of them and speak to him. Would you like (to
possess the) riches and nobility? Upon thee (be) the curse of

---

[1] upon that.   [2] narrowed from the secret of himself.   [3] suffice
you against M.   [4] Thornton, §§ 446–470, 482.   [5] upon.   [6] pf.

God. Ill is the man thou (art). This (comes) of your opinion.
What you will, then it is yours. Every act which brings near
the owner of it to[1] God, then it is piety. Thy preserving of
thy secret is more necessary than the preserving it of other
than thee. Many a word plunders affluence. Do not think
humble the sound opinion from the humble man, for the pearl
is not to be despised for the slightness of its diver. Then he
said, Verily no one will (one will not) be present at a time like
this (on the like of this day). The book is being sold for thirty
piastres standard.

18. Nominal Sentences[2].

Verily God—exalted be He—is one. He is the first and the
last, the outward and the inward. The wonder is not from my
love for Thee, and I am a poor slave ; but the wonder is from
Thy love for me, and Thou art a powerful king. Verily the
prayer is the tent-pole of the religion. The bane of the science
is the forgetting ; the bane of manhood is the breaking of the
promise. Verily, the fleet horse sometimes stumbles. Verily a
better than the good is the doer of it. Verily thou wilt not
gather from the thistles the grapes. The first of anger is
madness, and the end of it is remorse. The wisdom is the erring
(she-camel) of the believer. The medicine of the times is the
patience upon them. Evil, its little is much. In the hurry is the
repenting, and in the acting slowly is the salvation. Every
prevented (thing is) being followed. Muchness of laughter
makes to go away veneration. The promise of the generous is a
debt. One day to the learned is better than the life all of it to
the ignorant. The advice, in it is a blessing. Verily the man
excels the woman in the strength of the body, but she excels him
in the strength of the endurance. Know that to the works is a
reward. The remonstrance is the soap of the hearts.

[1] from.   [2] Thornton, §§ 512–533.

19. CONDITIONAL AND HYPOTHETICAL SENTENCES[1].

When you want that you should be obeyed, then ask what is able to be done. If there be not agreeing (with), then parting. He who loves a thing makes much from the mention of it. Sleep safe, you will be in the smoothest of beds. He who is pleased with his own opinion errs. He who does not ride the terrors, does not acquire the objects of desire. If you exaggerate in counsel, it will rush with you upon shame. If there become your guest a disliked (one), then entertain him with patience. When you return from a journey, then present to your people even if (it were) a stone. If you do not wink upon the mote you will never be satisfied. Make less thy food, thou wilt praise thy sleep. He who seeks a thing and exerts himself, finds. He who approves an ugly (thing), then he has already worked it. What would you do if you owned a million dollars? Stretch out your hand and I will swear[2] allegiance to you. He who acts slowly gets what he feels a desire for. If you are in need of one to send, send a wise (man) and do not give him any charge[3]. He who conceals his secret attains his wished. If you see me in some of my messages vie in excellence between party and party and balance between policy and policy, then know that I write what I write in the name of (the) virtue, not in the name of (the) policy. If it were decreed to each one of us that he should work (at) what he wills the course[4] and progress of the world would come to a standstill. We had not sat this sitting had we resolved to[5] disobey you. Obey him who is above you, (and) he who is below you will obey you.

---

[1] Thornton, §§ 587–590. [2] apoc. [3] charge him.
[4] travelling. [5] and in our resolution that we should.

20. Miscellaneous Sentences.

1. Two will not be satiated, a seeker of science and a seeker of money.   2. The outward of the remonstrance is better than the inward of the rancour.   3. The heart of the stupid is in his mouth and the tongue of the intelligent is in his heart.   4. It is not of the custom of the generous, the putting off of the showing favour.   5. Verily the wise man when he wishes an affair consults in regard to it the men, even if he were knowing, well informed.   6. Between the drowning in (the) praise and the drowning in (the) blame, (the) reality dies a death, there is no life to it from after it.   7. It was said to Al-Hajjaj, What is patience? He said the repressing of (the) rage and the endurance of what is not wished.   8. When the kings object to (the) justice, the subjects object to (the) obedience.   9. The stumble of the foot is better than the stumble of the tongue.   10. Verily (the war) will rub you with the rubbing of the handmill on its apron.   11. Whatever of disposition is with (before) a man, even if he fancied it to be concealed from (upon) men, will be known.   12. We have filled the land until it is too narrow for us (has narrowed from us), and the back of the sea, we will fill it with ships : to us belongs this world and those who are (in the forenoon) upon it.   13. And I know that he who survives longest (the living remaining) of men is unto a term of which the furthest reach is near.   14. When we parted it was as if I and Malik, for (all) the length of union, had not passed a night[1] together.   15. Verily the Fates, their arrows do not go wide.   16. The soul is desiring eagerly when thou makest it to desire eagerly, and when it is turned back to a little (few) it is content.   17. The souls of the creatures long for (the month of) May, and the longing is only for (unto) its rose.   18. I sometimes go out in the morning when (and) the birds are in their nests.

[1] acc.

19. If this world were to be sold I would buy him with it. 20. I passed the night watching Orion until there gradually draws near [to the west] from its first [stars] a sloping. 21. This book, if it be looked at with the eye of equity, will be seen (to be) more useful than the Hamasa. 22. The king when he is empty of (the) science is like the excited elephant, it does not pass a thing except it stamp on it. 23. Al-Mamun was clement, beautiful of (the) relenting, known for (by) that. 24. So when there reached him this saying, he did not exceed upon that he said, May God curse (fight) him, how violent is his invective. 25. And were it not for the fearing of prolixity (the making long), I would indeed mention a company from the clement ones of the kings in this place. 26. Al-Mustansir was more generous than the wind, but where is his bounty from (compared with) that of Kan? 27. To sin along with (the) advice is more sound than the correct along with the being single and the being despotic. 28. It is not for the king that he should be rancorous, and it is not for him that he should take oath when he tells news. 29. And of the items the want of which is desirable in the king are the being annoyed and the loathing and the boredom, for that is the most harming of the affairs, and the most corrupting to his state. 30. Zuhair said : I loathe the troubles (ceremonies) of life, and he who has gained a livelihood for eighty rounds (you have no father !) loathes ; and Kaab the son of Zuhair said : Every son of womankind, even if long were his weal, some day upon a hump-backed instrument (i.e. a bier) is to be borne. 31. The resemblance of those who boast themselves in what is transient is as the resemblance of those who boast themselves in what they see in the sleeping. 32. A man said to Abu'l-Darda : What ails us[1], we dislike death ? Then he said, Because you have ruined your next world and cultivated your this world. So you dislike that you should transport yourselves from the cultivation to the ruin. 33. Ali ibn abi Talib, when he entered a cemetery[2], used to say, The

[1] is to us.   [2] the tomb.

peace upon you, O people of the desolate dwellings ! 34. The resemblance of the mean rich is like the resemblance of the mules and the donkeys (which) carry the gold and the silver and feed on the chopped straw and the barley. He whose interior is whole, his exterior is sound. 35. And as for the virtue of the books, then they have said that the book, it is the intimate who is not hypocritical and is not bored and does not remonstrate with you when you are rude to him and does not disclose your secret. 36. They say that the jugglers, when they wish that they should bewitch the eyes of men, place in the roof of a room a piece of (the) loadstone and on its floor[1] another piece ; thereafter they leave (alone) in the open a piece of (the) iron, which does not cease preponderating alternately between these (two) attracting (forces). 37. Four things are a fatal poison and four things are their antidote : this world is a fatal poison and (the) abstinence in regard to it is its antidote, and money is a fatal poison and charity is its antidote, and speech is a fatal poison and the mention of God is its antidote, and the property of this world is a fatal poison and justice is its antidote. 38. It was said to a madman : Reckon for us the madmen ; he said : This will be long with me, but I will reckon the intelligent. 39. It was said to Lokman : How ugly is your face ! he said : Do you lay the defect of this painting upon me, or upon the painter ? 40. A man said to Euclid the sage : I will not rest until I cause you to perish[2] ; he said : and I will not rest until I make to go out the rancour from your heart. 41. Al-Muhallab said to his sons, O my sons, when you stop in the markets, then do not stop except by (upon) him who sells (the) arms or sells (the) books. 42. Muawiya said, How ugly in the king is that he should exaggerate in the acquisition (making to result) of any science (a science of the sciences). 43. Some people think (Of them are those who were seeing good) that (the) rancour is a praiseworthy item in the king. 44. Buzurjumihr said, It is desirable that the king should be more rancorous than a camel ; and I—I differ in regard

[1] earth.   [2] or I efface (*subj.*) your spirit.

19

to this saying. 45. It behoves that the king should be like the earth in the concealing of his secret, and like the fire upon the people of corruption, and like the water in his softness to those who deal softly with him. 46. And it behoves that he be quicker of hearing than a mare, and more keensighted than an eagle, and better guided than a kata, and more wary (more violent in being ware) than a crow, and more venturesome (mightier in venturesomeness) than the lion, and stronger and swifter than the panther. 47. Saladin Yusuf ibn Aiyub (Joseph son of Job) master of Egypt and Syria was very indulgent, which was his chief characteristic (much of indulgence, described by it). 48. Omar son of Al-Khattab said to a man, Verily I do not love you. He said, Then you make defective from my due somewhat (a thing). Omar said, No. The man said, Then there will not rejoice in love after this except the women. 49. One of the wise of the Persians said, The cares of the people (men) are small, and the cares of the kings are great. 50. Sovereignty is a bride whose dowries are the souls. 51. Muawiya looked at the army of the commander of the faithful, Ali (upon him be peace), at Siffin : then he turned to Amr son of Al-As and said, He who seeks a mighty (thing) stakes (with) a mighty. 52. Of the advantages of acting slowly and deliberately is the security from remorse (at the time) when remorse does not avail. 53. There does not behove (to) the perfect man except that he should be in the furthest goal from the seeking of the sovereignty or in the furthest goal from the leaving it alone. 54. And similarly it does not behove (to) him that his boast should be in the fathers and the grandfathers, and only it behoves that his boast should be in the virtues which he (has) made to result. 55. The Persians say, The corruption of the kingdom and the becoming bold of the subjects and the ruin of the country is in the rendering vain of the promise and the threat. 56. One of the wise said, A sultan whose subjects fear him is better than a sultan who fears his subjects. 57. And here is the place for (of) a story, there is no harm in setting it down (making

it to go down):—Harun al-Rashid entered upon one of the
ascetics, then he saluted him : then he said, And upon thee be
the peace : O king, dost thou love God? He said, Yes. He said,
Then dost thou disobey Him ? He said, Yes. He said, Thou
liest, by Allah, in regard to thy loving Him ; verily thou, if thou
lovedst Him, wouldest not disobey Him. 58. And of the
items which it is desirable that they should be in the king is
(the) liberality, and it is the root in making to incline to him the
hearts, and obtaining good advice (making to result the counsels)
from the world and taking into service the nobles. 59. Verily
death in the seeking of glory is better than life along with
abasement. 60. Ibn Muljam (God curse him) was arrested
and imprisoned until it should be looked what should be of the
affair of Ali (God be satisfied with (from) him). 61. One of
the rich boasted himself to one of the wise in his fathers and
grandfathers and in the tinsels of the corruptible money. Then
said to him that wise one, If in these things were a boast, then
it behoves that the boast should be to them not to you ; and if
your fathers were, as you mention, nobles, then the boast is to
them not to you. 62. Do not indeed think small the affair of
your enemy when you war with him, because you, if you are
victorious over him, will not be praised[1], and if he be victorious
over you, you will not be excused[1]. 63. How beautiful is the
saying of Abu Nuwas to Harun al-Rashid : I had feared you :
thereafter there made me safe from that I should fear you, your
fearing God. 64. And Harun al-Rashid was not fearing God
but Abu Nuwas ran (flowed) in his saying upon the custom of the
poets. 65. Preachers (the calling ones) are the most needy of
men unto firm resolutions and hearts patient upon the endurance
of calamities and trials. 66. Many (much from) men will say,
What does his call avail the caller in a nation which does not
make good about him a thinking, and does not hear to him a
saying ? 67. This is what Satan whispers with to the incapable
and the ignorant, and verily ignorance is a thick covering which

---

[1] apoc.

covers the intellect and knowledge (science). 68. The ignorant are sick and the learned are physicians. 69. (It is)
absurd (to suppose) that there should pull down the building of
the false, one individual in one age. 70. He who knows not
truth and false stamps with the stamping of the blind she-
camel. 71. There is not got up an exhibition in which are
exhibited the dogs in England except and there is present at it
the King and Queen of England, or they send from their dogs to
it the most excellent of the kinds. 72. And to the English
from their King to their private persons is a perfect care in the
health of their dogs. 73. It happened that his dog Caesar
(Emperor) was sick and immediately he sent a telegram to the
physician, and described the symptoms (accidents) of the disease,
then the physician sent the explanation of the treatment by wire
(upon the tongue of the lightning). 74. The noble women of
the Franks have not left alone a way except they have taken it,
in endeavouring after (behind) the assembling of the money and
the doing of the good. 75. The duchess said, Verily I am
longing for (unto) the happy day in which the women will desist
from employing the feathers of birds as an ornament to the head,
so that these beautiful birds may be reared (trained) in order
that the world may be ornamented by them. 76. I went to
Jiddah in these days on my way to Medina the Illumined with
the object of the visitation of the grave of the Elect One (upon
him prayer and peace). 77. As soon as (the first of what) my
feet trod its soil I saw a friend who clave to me much in my
numerous journeys, and, after that he pointed me upon a place
which I might hire, I began to be interested in the study of the
states of the city and the knowledge of the characters and
customs of its people and the amount of their fortune from the
social life. 78. And the great (mighty) mass [of the people]
there look down on (think humble) him who inclines to (the)
science and despise him and look at him as they look at a
criminal. 79. And the state of tyranny (wronging) has
arrived at a degree that he takes on every ship a third of what
it makes to result, and on the camel 10 dollars, and upon the

mare or horse 20 dollars, and thus upon every thing. 80. And as for the folk themselves (their souls), then they are folk in the extreme (end) of meekness and softness : they do not know (the) evil and are not familiar with (the) treachery ; and were it not for that, no one would (one would not) put himself in possession of despotism (of that he should be despotic) to this extent (limit). 81. Then he said, This question, you will find its answer with other than me ; and as for me, it is not for me that I should wade in the like of this. 82. We do not anticipate (think there will befall) a happy future for Nejd as long as its people (are) distant from the meeting places of the sciences and the arts. 83. The question which has occupied Egypt (the Egyptian district) from one end of it to the other (from its furthest to its furthest) long days has come to an end. 84. And the grace of the Khedive has (Khedivial graces have) necessitated that it should be forgiven to all of the students against (upon) whom there was proved (made firm) the transgression in the past events. 85. And they assert that these three (men) had taken in hand the beating of the students upon their feet with the bastinado (in the stocks). 86. Verily this telegram is not from the son of Al-Rashid, because he—there does not remain of the family of Al-Rashid one besides a lad who has not passed (on) the seventh (year) from his age. 87. In India and in (the) particular in Bombay are many of (much from) the Arabs dependents (to) the High Government (Daulah) : then of them are those who traffic in (the) horses, of the people of Bagdad and Al-Mausil and Al-Basrah and Al-Zubeir, and of them those who traffic in (the) pearls, of the peoples of Oman and Al-Bahrein (the two seas) and Katar and Nejd and Al-Kuweit ; and of them those residing (the ones dwelling) as correspondents (for the traffic correspondences) between Al-Irak and Egypt and the Hijaz and Europe. 88. They say that the science of the religions and the science of the bodies are (two) brothers. Then if the body and apparel of the man be clean his worship[1] is correct and his health is good and his intercourse is pleasant

[1] inf.

(nice). 89. Is the man able that he should be a politician except when he knows that between his (two) sides is a heart petrified, there does not agitate it the being distressed of the distressed, nor disquiet it the adversities of those smitten with adversity? 90. They say that politics is not a science from the sciences which the man learns in school or studies in a book, and it is only a miscellany of thoughts, of which the code is (the) experiments and its basis (the) practice. 91. Every man complains and says that he is engaged upon work other than corresponding to his nature and his inclinations, and that he, if they let him choose, would arrange his life with an arranging which would disagree from its present state of things. 92. Verily the most of men work useful works by reason of their being forced into the work with the being forced [into the death] of one desiring eagerly (the) life. 93. And, alas[1], you will not find one from them who has assisted upon interests in which are benefits to them and to the Moslems, in the construction of a mosque or a school or the assisting of a railway. 94. This paper (leaf) is an Arabic, patriotic, daily, political, commercial (traffic), critical, humorous newspaper, and its name is 'The Sun of the Truth (Reality).' 95. There have appeared (come up) from this newspaper until (the) now three numbers, which the newspapers have eulogised in few words and lines reckoned upon the fingers of the one hand, as if it were a weekly newspaper of no consequence (no importance to it) which had appeared (come up) in one of the villages of the country districts. 96. And I do not purpose the making to overflow in the eulogising it because the newspaper of the 'Sun of the Truth (Reality)' is more excellent than the rest of the papers (pages), nor because it is more chaste in language or (and) more full of news (more of narratives): not this and not that; for it is a small paper (page), its bulk does not exceed upon the bulk of one page from one of the numbers of the 'Muaiyad.' Verily the reason (respect) of my being interested in it is other than this:

[1] for the grief.

It is the first newspaper which has appeared in Mecca the Honoured, in the city of the Koran, in the mother of the villages. 97. He who circumambulates the land of Al-Irak, of the engineers of the irrigation, is not slow to (does not tarry that he should) perceive (feel) the mighty difference between the delta of the Nile and the delta of the two rivers (of the) Tigris and the Euphrates. 98. For the increase of the Nile appears in August and goes on until (unto) the month of October, and in the course of this space the waters, mingled with the silt, cover the land of Egypt. Thereafter they subside from it and return to the bed (flow) of the river in November. And at that time they scatter the land with the winter sowing (agriculture), as the wheat and the barley and the beans and the clover. As to in the country of what is between the two rivers, then verily the increase makes a beginning in (the) Tigris and the Euphrates from the month of March and continues (abides) until (unto) the month of May. Thereafter comes a season in which the heat (of summer) becomes violent, and in which the rains are imprisoned, and that continues (abides) in June and July and August; and in this time the seed will be in need of (unto) the water. 99. Do not wonder if I say that (the) sagacity is other than the intellect, for (then) the thieves and the liars and the hypocrites are sagacious, and there is not among them one intelligent (person), for they make themselves (their souls) to go down the wateringplaces of ruin and perdition. 100. The snow has been (is) alighting in England since six days and its average thickness (the average of its thickness) is six inches, and news is to hand (there go down the narratives) concerning the violent storms and the heaping up of the snows from all of the directions of Europe. 101. Our sufficiency is God and good is the Agent.

PART II

EASIER PROSES

1. Culprit and Sultan.

A culprit[1] entered one day upon a sultan. Then he said to
him, With what face do you meet me? Then he said, With the
face with which I shall meet God, and my crimes towards Him
are mightier, and His punishment greater. So he forgave him.

MUSTA'SIMI.

2. In regard to Wine.

A man left alone the fermented drink. Then it was said to
him, Why have you left it alone, and it is the apostle of gladness
unto the heart? He said, But it is an ill apostle: it is sent to
the belly and it goes to the head.

SHARĪSHI.

3. The Educating of the Old Man.

A man looked at a philosopher educating an old man, then
said to him, What are you performing? He said, Washing an
Abyssinian, perchance he may become white.

MUSTA'SIMI.

4. Alexander and his Namesake.

Alexander saw a namesake of his not ceasing being routed in
the wars. Then he said to him: O you there[2], either change[3]
your action or change your name.

MUSTA'SIMI.

[1] owner of a fault.   [2] O this.   [3] either that you change.

5. The King and his Slave.

A king sent to a slave of his: What ails you[1], you do not serve me, and you are my slave? Then he answered him: If you reflected, you would know that you are the slave of my slave, because you follow passion: so you are its slave; and I rule[2] it, so it is my slave.

MUSTA' SIMI.

6. The Sage and the Flame.

A sage asked a lad with whom was a torch: From where comes the fire after that it is extinguished. Then he said: If you will inform me to where it goes I will inform you from where it comes.

Latā'if al-Wuzara.

7. Hunter and Bird.

A hunter was hunting the (little) birds on a cold day. Then he was slaughtering them, and the tears were pouring. Then said a (little) bird to his companion: No harm upon you from the man; do you not see him weeping? Then said to him the other: Do not look at his tears, but at what his hands perform.

SHARĪSHI.

8. The Deposed Wali.

Al-Jahiz says: I entered upon Mohammad son of Isaac commander of Bagdad in the days of his waliship and he (was) sitting in the divan and the people[3] (were a) standing to receive orders before him[4] as if over their heads (were) the birds[5]. Thereafter I entered in to him after a space, and he (had been) deposed, and he was sitting and around him the books and notebooks and inkhorns and rulers. Then I did not see him more venerable than he (was) in that state.

Al-Fakhri.

[1] What is to you.   [2] own.   [3] men.
[4] between his hands.   [5] i.e. with gravity and expectancy.

9. KHALIF AND VICEROY.

Marwan, the last of the kings of the Beni[1] Umaiyah, wrote to[2] a viceroy of his who had presented to[2] him a black lad, then said: If you had known a number less than one and a colour worse than the black, you would indeed have presented it; and farewell.

Latā'if al-Wuzara.

10. THE TWO COMFORTERS.

Wasif the Turk wali of Syria—there hit him a calamity, so there rode to him Mohammad al-Zaiyat. Then he comforted him with narratives and proverbs. Next Mohammad was struck by a calamity, then there rode to him Wasif, then said to him: O Abu[3] Jaafar, I am a man, an alien: I do not know what I shall say to you, but look what you comforted me with that day and comfort with it yourself now. Then the people thought fine his speech.

Latā'if al-Wuzara.

11. AL-RASHID AND HUMAID.

Al-Rashid was angry with[4] Humaid of Tus, then he ordered for him the leather-carpet[5] and the sword. Then he wept. Then he said to him, What makes you weep? Then he said, By Allah, O Commander of the Believers I am not nervous about[6] death, for, as for it, there is no escape from it, and I only wept out of grief at[4] my going out from the world, whilst[7] the Commander of the Believers is displeased with[4] me. So he laughed and forgave him.

IBSHAIHI.

---

[1] sons of.　　[2] unto.　　[3] father of.　　[4] upon.　　[5] called for him with the leather-carpet (on which to behead him).　　[6] from.
[7] and.

12. MOHAMMAD AL-ZAIYAT.

It is said that Mohammad the Oilseller worked an oven of
iron and placed nails in the inside of it in order that he might
punish whomsoever he wanted to punish. Then he was the first
who was put into it, and it was said to him : Taste what you
desired that you should make people taste.

Al-Fakhri.

13. JAAFAR AND HIS LAD.

It is related concerning Jaafar the Truthful that a lad of his
stood (still) to pour the water upon his hands. Then the jug fell
from the hand of the lad into the basin. Then the drops flew
into his face. Then Jaafar looked at him with the look of one
made angry. Then he said, O my patron, God commands (with)
the repressing of rage. He said, I have forgiven (from) you.
He said, And God loves those who do good. He said, Go, for
you are free for the sake of God—exalted be He.

IBSHAIHI.

14. THE KHALIF BECOMES WATCHMAN.

Abd al-Rahman the son of Auf said : Omar the son of
Al-Khattab called me one night and said : There has alighted at
the gate of the City a caravan, and I fear for them when they
sleep that (some) thing should be stolen from their belongings.
So I passed (away) along with him. Then when we arrived he
said to me : Sleep you. Then verily he began keeping watch
over the caravan the whole night[1].

GHAZĀLI.

[1] the length of his night.

15. STRANGE JUSTICE.

A woman came to a kadi, then said : My husband died and left (alone) his parents and children and a wife[1] and people, and to him (was) money. Then he said : To his parents the bereavement, and to his children the orphanhood, and to his wife the change (of husband), and to his people the fewness (of benefits) and the abasement. And the money will be carried to us, so that[2] there do not fall in regard to it between you the litigation.

THA'ĀLABI.

16. KISRA ANUSHIRWAN AND THE TEACHER.

It is narrated that Kisra Anushirwan—there was to him a teacher, fair of the educating, teaching[3] him until he was proficient in the sciences. Then the teacher beat him on a day for other than a fault, so Anushirwan harboured rancour against him. Then when he succeeded to the reign he said to the teacher, What instigated you upon beating me[4] such and such a day[5]? Then he said to him, When I saw you eagerly desirous[3] in the science, I hoped for the reign for you after your father. So I wished[6] that I should make you taste the flavour of wronging in order that you may not wrong. Then said Anushirwan, Bravo, Bravo ! and he elevated his value.

IBSHAIHI.

17. OMAR AND THE THUNDER.

Omar the son of Abd al-Aziz was stopping along with Solomon the son of Abd al-Malik the days of his caliphate, then he heard a voice of thunder. Then Solomon was nervous about[7] it and placed his breast upon the forepart of his saddle. Then said to him Omar : This is the voice of His mercy : then how (will be) the voice of His punishment ?

---

[1] woman. [2] until. [3] impf. [4] my beating. [5] day of so and so. [6] loved. [7] from.

18. THE INVITED TO THE FEAST AND THE BEGGAR.

A man invited another into his alighting place and said : Let us eat with you bread and salt. Then the man thought that that was a metonymy for[1] gentle pleasant food which the master of the alighting place had prepared, so he went with[2] him, and he offered him nothing beyond[3] the bread and salt. Then whilst they were eating, lo, there stopped at the door a beggar. Then the master of the alighting place drove him off often, then he was not chid away. So he said to him : Go away, and if not I will come out[4] to you and break[4] your head. Then said the invited : O you there, leave ! for you, if you knew of the veracity of his threat what I know of the veracity of his promise, you would not oppose yourself to him.

BAHĀ AL-DĪN.

19. YAZID AND THE BEDAWI WOMAN.

Yazid the son of Al-Muhallab was at his going out from the prison of Omar the son of Abd al-Aziz journeying in the wilds with his son Muawiya. Then he passed a Bedawi woman. Then she slaughtered for them a she-goat. Then when they two had eaten, Yazid said to his son, What will be with you of the expense ? He said : A hundred deniers. He said, Give her them. This is a poor (person) : the little will satisfy her, and she does not know you. He said : If the little were satisfying her, then I—there does not satisfy me save the much ; and if she were not knowing me, then I—I know myself.

IBN QUTAIBA.

[1] from. [2] passed away along with. [3] did not exceed upon.
[4] pf.

20. The Lad and his Uncle.

A lad of Hashim—his uncle wished that he should reward him for some foolishness he had done[1]. Then he said: O Uncle, verily I have done evil, and there is not to me an intellect; so do not you do evil, with an intellect like yours[2].

THA'ĀLABI.

21. The Short Flagellator.

It is related that a man of Medina was brought drunk to one of the walis. So he ordered the constituting of the legal punishment upon him. And the man was tall, and the flagellator was short, and could not reach up to beat him[3]. Then said the flagellator, Shorten yourself, so that the beating may get you. Then he said to him: Woe be to you, is it to the eating of sweatmeat you are inviting me? I would that I were taller than Og the son of Anak, and you shorter than Gog and Magog.

NAWĀJI.

22. The Astronomer and the Well.

One of the companions of Alexander said that an astronomer invited them one night that he might show them the stars and make them know their particularities and the conditions of their travelling. Then he made them enter into a plantation, and began walking with them and pointing with his hand to them until he tumbled into a well there. Then he said: Whoever is devoted to the science of what is above him is tried by what is beneath him.

BAHĀ AL-DĪN.

[1] a folly from him.   [2] and to you is your intellect.
[3] did not put himself in possession of his beating.

23. Forgiveness.

Blood[1] fell between two tribes of Koreish. Then came in Abu
Sufyan, then there did not remain one lowering[2] his head except
he elevated it. Then he said, O congregation of Koreish, would
you like what is right or[3] what is more excellent than the
right? They said, And is there a thing more excellent than the
right? Then he said : Yes, the forgiveness. Then the folk lost
no time, then made peace with one another.

SHARĪSHI.

24. Omar and the Lad.

It is said that Omar the son of Abd al-Aziz was looking by
night into the matters concerning his[4] subjects by[5] the light of a
lamp[6]. Then came to him a lad of his, then told him news about
some business[7] which was connected with his own[8] house. Then
Omar said to him, Extinguish the lamp[6], afterwards tell me the
news, for this oil is from the treasury[9] of the Muslims, and it is
not permitted to use it save in the business of the Muslims.

GHAZĀLI.

25. The Forgiveness of Abd al-Malik.

The Khalif Abd al-Malik fell into a rage against Raja the son
of Hayah, then said : By Allah, indeed if God puts me in
possession of him, I will verily indeed do with him so and so.
Then when he came before him[10], Raja the son of Hayah said to
him : O Commander of the Believers, God hath performed what
you wished[11], so perform what God wishes[11]. So he forgave him,
and ordered for him a gratuity.

IBSHAIHI.

[1] pl.　　　[2] placing.　　　[3] is there to you in the right or in.
[4] the tales of the.　　[5] in.　　[6] torch.　　[7] in the meaning of a cause.
[8] that is, Omar's.　　[9] house of the money.　　[10] between his hands.
[11] loved.

26. THE SLAVEGIRL AND THE DISH.

There came a slavegirl belonging to Jaafar with a dish of panada to proffer it to him, and with him were folk. Then she hastened with it : then it tumbled from her hand : then it broke : then there hit him and his companions some of what was in it : then the slavegirl was frightened at that : then he said to her : You are free for the sake of God—exalted be He. Perchance it (is the case) that it will be a compensation for the fright which hit you.

TURTŪSHI.

27. THE DOG AND THE DRUM.

It is related that a dog—there was of its custom when it heard the voice of a drum in a place it would go to it thinking that in it is a wedding or a feast. Then worked the people a trick upon that dog, and they agreed together that they should beat the drum in two villages ; as often as the dog came to the beating-place of the drum, it would be silenced and beaten in the other village. So they did that. Then began the dog running between the two villages : as often as it came to a village of them, they silenced the drum and it was beaten in the other village. And it did not cease like that until the dog died, hungry, thirsty.

SUYŪTI.

28. THE FOX AND THE COCK.

It is related that the fox passed in the early morning by a tree. Then he saw above it a cock. So he said to him : Will you not alight that we may say prayers in common? Then he said : Verily the imám is sleeping behind the tree, so awake him. Then the fox looked, then he saw the dog and he turned fleeing. Then called to him the cock. Do you not come that we may say prayers ? Then he said: My ablution has been invalidated, so have patience until I renew to me an ablution and return.

SUYŪTI.

29. YAHYA THE SON OF KHALID AND THE SIGNET-RING.

It was said to Yahya the son of Khalid the son of Barmak :
O (the) Wazeer, inform us of the best of what you saw in the
days of your felicity. Then he said : I embarked one day (upon
one of the days) on a ship intending to picnic[1]. And there was
upon my finger a ring. Then its stone flew from my hand, and
it was a red hyacinth, its value a thousand *mithkals* of the gold.
Then I drew an ill omen from that. Thereafter I returned to
my lodging[2], and, lo, the cook had come with that very stone[3]
and said : O (the) Wazeer, I met this stone in the belly of a fish ;
and that was because I bought fish for the kitchen, then split their
belly. Then I saw this stone. Then I said : This is not fit[4]
except for the Wazeer—may God—exalted be He—make him
great[5]. Said Yahya : Then I said, The praise be to God, this is
the attaining of the goal.

ITLĪDI.

30. KEEPING[6] OF THE TONGUE.

It has reached us that two men met together. Then said one
of them to his companion : How many have you found in the
son of Adam of the defects ? He said : They are more than that
they should be presented ; and I have found a thing[7], if the man
use it, it will veil the defects, all of them. He said : What is it ?
He said : Keeping[6] of the tongue.

IBSHAIHI.

31. BLIND MAN AND CRIPPLE.

Verily a blind (man) and a cripple were in a village in
poverty and distress[8]. There was none leading the blind nor
any carrying the cripple. And there was in the village a man
who was feeding them in every day out of disinterestedness with
their nourishment from the food and the drink. Then they did
not cease (being) in welfare until the disinterested (person)

---

[1] inf.   [2] alightingplace.   [3] that stone with its eye.
[4] sound.   [5] pf.   [6] preserving.   [7] an item.   [8] harm.

perished. Then they stayed after he was dead[1] (some) days : then their hunger became violent and the pangs reached from them their utmost height. So they united their opinion upon that the blind should carry the cripple. Then the cripple will indicate the way by his sight, and the blind will be independent by the carrying of the cripple, and they two will go round in the village begging food of its people. So they did so ; then their affair succeeded ; and if they had not done it, they would have perished.

TURTŪSHI.

32. THE MAN AND DEATH.

A man once carried a bundle of fuel : then it was heavy upon him. Then when he was tired and annoyed from carrying it, he threw it down and imprecated death upon himself[2]. Then Death presented himself to him, saying : Here I am, for what did you summon me ? Then said to him the man : I summoned you that you might transfer this bundle of fuel upon my shoulder.

The moral of it.—That the world in its entirety loves this world, and is only bored from weakness and misery.

LOKMĀN.

33. THE KEEPING OF THE SECRET.

One of the men told as a secret to a man talk and commanded him to keep it secret[3]. Then when the talk was finished, he said to him : Do you understand ? He said : Nay, I am ignorant. Thereafter he said to him : Do you remember ?[4] He said : Nay, I have forgotten.

And Amr the son of Al-As said : If I divulge my secret to my friend, (and) he then reveals it, the blame is upon me not upon him. It was said to him : And how (is) that ? He said : Because I should have kept it more[5] than he.

THA'ĀLABI.

---

[1] after him.   [2] called against his spirit with death.   [3] conceal.
[4] Have you preserved ?   [5] I was more deserving of keeping it safe.

34. THE ARAB AND THE MOON.

It is related that an Arab lost[1] the way. Then he died of
vexation and made sure of perdition. Then when the moon was
gone up he was guided and found the way. Then he raised up
to it his head that he might thank it. Then he said to it: By
Allah, I know not what I shall say to you nor what I shall say
about you. Shall I say, May God exalt[2] you?—then God has
already exalted[3] you. Or shall I say, May God illumine you?—
then God has already illumined you. Or shall I say, May God
beautify you?—then God has already beautified you. But there
only remains the prayer that God would grant a delay in your
(appointed) term, even if He should make me from the evil your
redemption.

SHARĪSHI.

35. THE HOUSE-MOUSE AND THE MOUSE OF THE WILDERNESS.

It is said that[4] the mouse of the houses saw the mouse of the
wilderness in adversity[5] and trial. So she said to her, What are
you doing[6] here? Come[7] away with me to the house, in which
are (all) sorts of delight and plenty. So she went away with her
and, lo, the owner of the house in which she was dwelling had
fitted out for her the trap—a brick beneath which was a piece of
suet. So she rushed blindly in to seize the suet and there fell
upon her the brick and crushed her flat. So the desert mouse
fled, and shook her head, wondering to herself, and said: I see
much affluence and a violent proving. Verily, the welfare and
poverty are dearer to me than riches in which is death. Thereafter she fled to the wilds.

IBSHAIHI.

---

[1] caused to err. [2] raise up. [3] raised up. [4] verily. [5] violence.
[6] performing. [7] Go.

36. COUNSEL AND ADVICE.

Verily the wise man, when he wants an affair, consults in regard to it the men, even if he were knowing, well-informed. For he who is pleased with his own opinion errs, and he who thinks himself rich in his own intellect slips. Al-Hasan said : Men are three ; then a man is a man, and a man is half a man, and a man is not a man. Then as for the man (who is) the man, he is the possessed of the opinion and the advice. And as to the man who is half a man, it is he who has an opinion, but does not consult. And as to the man who is not a man, it is he who has not an opinion and does not consult.

IBSHAIHI.

37. AL-JAHIZ.

Some folk knocked at the door of[1] Al-Jahiz, then went out a boy of his. Then they asked him, What is he doing? Then he said, He is lying against God. It was said, How? He said : He looked into the mirror then said, The praise be to God who created me and made beautiful[2] my figure.

KAMĀL AL-DĪN AL-HALABI.

38. THE VISITOR[3] AND THE SICK.

A friend of Al-Hamid the son of Al-Abbas was sick. Then he wished to send[4] his son to visit him. Then he charged him and said : When you enter, then sit in the most elevated of the place and say to the sick, What do you complain of? Then when he says, So and so, then say : [You will soon be] free [of it], please God![5] And say to him, Who[6] comes to you of the physicians? Then when he says, Such a one, then say, a blessed, auspicious one. And say to him, What is your nutriment? Then when he says, So and so, then say, Admirable food.

[1] knocked the door upon.   [2] good.   [3] pc.   [4] fling.   [5] Safe, if God will.   [6] What.

So the son went and entered upon the invalid, and there was
before him[1] a lamp-stand, so he sat upon it on account of its
elevation : then it tumbled upon the breast of the invalid, then
hurt him. Thereafter he sat (down). Then he said to the
invalid : What do you complain of? Then he said with
impatience : I complain of the illness of death. Then he said :
[You will soon be] free [of it], please God[2]. He said, Then who
comes to you of the physicians ? He said, The Angel of Death.
He said, A blessed, auspicious one. He said, Then what is your
nutriment ? Then he said, The poison of death. He said,
Nice, admirable food.

KAMĀL AL-DĪN AL-HALABI.

39. VERACITY AND FALSEHOOD.

Verily veracity is the pillar of religion, and the corner of
education and the root of manhood. Then these three are not
complete except by it. And Aristotle said : The best of speech
is that in which the sayer of it is truth-speaking, and by which
the hearer of it is benefited. Verily death along with veracity is
better than life along with falsehood. And of what comes in this
subject[3] is the saying of Mahmud al-Warraq : Truth is a means
of deliverance to its lords, and a relationship which makes to
approach to the Lord.

IBSHAIHI.

40. SOLOMON AND THE ANGEL OF DEATH.

The Angel of Death entered one day in to Solomon when
there was in his assembly[4] a man of the children[5] of Israel.
Then the Angel of Death began making long the look towards
that man. Then the man was nervous at him. Then when the
Angel of Death had gone out from being with Solomon, then said
the man, O prophet of God, verily I wish that you would
command the wind to carry me to the country of India. So

[1] between his hands. [2] Safe, if God will. [3] door. [4] sitting. [5] sons.

Solomon commanded the wind, then it carried him off and placed him in the land of India. Thereafter the Angel of Death entered upon Solomon after that. Then said Solomon, O Angel of Death, verily the man at whom you were making long the look asked me that I should command the wind to carry him to the land of India, when he saw you making long the look at him. Then said the Angel of Death, O prophet of God, verily I was making long the look at him, because God—exalted be He—had commanded me to gather his spirit in the country of India : so when I saw him in your assembly[1], I wondered to myself at[2] that. Then when I went out from being with you, then I alighted upon the land of India, then I found the wind had carried him to there ; so I gathered his spirit. Then Solomon wondered in himself at[2] that.

41. Letter of Omar ibn al-Khattab to Amr ibn al-As.

Verily I praise unto thee God, except whom there is no god. To proceed : Then I have wondered at the muchness of my letters unto thee about thy making delay in the poll-tax and thy letter unto me concerning trifles[3]. And thou hast known that I am not satisfied from thee except with the clear truth. And I did not advance thee to Egypt to make it to thee a meal nor to thy folk. But I directed thee for what I hoped of thy enlarging the poll-tax, and the goodness of thy policy. Then when my letter comes to thee, carry the poll-tax, for it is only the booty[4] of the Muslims, and with me those whom thou knowest are a folk reduced to straits. Farewell.

42. Answer of Amr ibn al-'As.

To proceed : Now there has come to me the letter of the Commander of the Believers thinking me delaying in the poll-tax, and he asserts that I am swerving from the truth and am turning aside from the way. And verily I, by Allah, am not objecting to

[1] sitting. [2] from. [3] the little daughters of the roads. [4] shade.

the good of what thou knowest, but the people of the land asked
me for a postponement until their crops should mature. Then I
was considerate[1] to the Muslims, then the indulgence towards
them was better than that it should be dealt rashly with them,
then we should come[2] to what there is no dispensation[3] in them
from. Farewell.

SUYŪTI.

43. AL-RASHID AND THE SIGNET-RING.

A curious thing which happened[4] to Harun al-Rashid was
that his brother Musa al-Hadi, when he succeeded to the
Caliphate, asked about a signet-ring mighty of worth[5] which had
belonged to his father Al-Mahdi. Then it reached him that
Al-Rashid his brother had taken it. So he sought it from him.
Then he declined to give it to him. So he insisted upon him in
regard to it. Then Al-Rashid was enraged against him, and he
passed over the bridge of Bagdad and threw it into the Tigris.
Then when Al-Hadi died and Al-Rashid succeeded to the
Caliphate he came to that very place[6] and with him a signet-
ring of lead. So he threw it into that place and commanded
the divers to seek it, so they dived for it and extracted the first
ring. Then Al-Rashid was gladdened and reckoned that of his
felicity and of the prolonging[7] of his reign.

ABU'L FARAJ.

44. SALADIN AND THE WOMAN WHO HAD LOST HER CHILD[8].

Saladin was a perfect imam. There did not become wali of
Egypt after the Companions the like of him, not before him nor
after him. And he was very gentle of heart and men were safe
from his oppression on account of his justice. And of his doings[9]
is what Al-'Imad relates, as follows[10]: There had been to the

[1] looked.　　[2] become.　　[3] riches.　　[4] Of the strange of what
occurred.　　[5] value.　　[6] that place in its eye.　　[7] making to remain.
[8] the missed, her child (gen.).　　[9] handicrafts.　　[10] has informed,
he said:

Muslims thieves who were entering by night the tents of the Franks, then were stealing. Then it occurred that one of them took a suckling boy three months old[1] from his cradle. Then his mother pined over him with a violent pining, and made complaint to their kings. Then they said to her : Verily the Sultan of the Muslims is merciful of heart, so go away to him. So she came to the Sultan Saladin, then wept and complained of the affair of her child. Then he was sorry for her with a violent sorrow[2] and his eyes wept. So he commanded to present her child. Then, lo, he was sold in the market. So he wrote officially for the handing of his price to the buyer, and he did not cease standing still until the child was brought. Then he handed him to his mother and carried her upon a mare to her folk with honour[3].

SUYŪTI.

45. Saladin and the King of England.

Then Saladin made preparations for the siege. Then there came on a deputation to him the messenger[4] of the Franks and the truce was knotted with them. And the reason of that was that the King of the English—his being absent had been long from his own country, and long had been the campaign. So he wrote to Al-Malik al-Adil asking him for the entering upon the Sultan : then the Sultan answered him (favourably) to that, and there agreed upon it the opinion of the commanders, for what had happened with the army of being annoyed and of the expenses being exhausted. Then they took oath mutually upon that, and the King of England did not take oath, but they took his hand and made a covenant with him. And he excused himself by (the fact) that kings do not take oath, and the Sultan was content with that. And the truce was upon (condition) that there should be settled in the hands of the Franks Jaffa and Cæsarea and Arsuf and Haifa and Acre with their dependencies,

---

[1] a son of three months.   [2] gentleness.   [3] honoured.   [4] apostle.

and that Ascalon should be dismantled[1], and permission was given[2] to the Franks in regard to the visitation of Jerusalem. And it was a famous day : there covered the men from both sides, of joy and gladness, what God only knows. And the King of England set out upon the sea, returning to his own town.

IBN SHĀZI.

46. THE INDULGENCE OF SALADIN.

He entered once into the bath following upon a long sickness which had made him weak and worn out his strength. So he was made to enter the bath and he was in an extreme from the weakness. Then he sought from a mameluke, who was stopping by (upon) his head, hot water. So he presented to him in a bowl water violent of (the) hotness. Then when he was near to (from) him, the hand of the mameluke shook (was troubled), so the bowl fell upon him, then the water burned his body. Then he did not chastise him, not even (and not) in speech. Thereafter he sought from him an hour after that (after that by an hour) cold water, so he presented to him in that bowl water violent of (the) cold. Then (at the time) when he was near to him, there occurred to him what occurred at the first time of the shaking (being troubled) of his hand and the falling of the bowl with that water violent of (the) cold. So he fainted and almost died. Then when he recovered, he said to the mameluke : If you want to kill me (If you were wishing my killing), then make me know (it). And he did not exceed upon this word—may He be satisfied with him.

Al-Fakhri.

47. THE DEATH OF YAZDAYARD.

Yazdayard came to Merv fleeing from Kirman, then he asked its marzuban and its people for money, then they refused (prevented) him and feared him and killed his companions ; and Yazdayard went out fleeing upon his feet, along with him his

[1] a ruin.   [2] it was allowed.

girdle and his sword and his crown, until he came to an end
at (unto) the dwelling (alightingplace) of a hewer of millstones
upon the bank of the Murghab. Then when Yazdayard was off
his guard (was negligent) the hewer of millstones killed him, and
took his belongings and cast his body in the Murghab. And
next morning (And there were in the morning) the people of
Merv, then they followed up his trace until it was concealed upon
them at the dwelling (alightingplace) of the hewer of millstones,
then they took him : then he confessed to them of (about) his
killing, and brought out (made to go out) his belongings. So
they killed the hewer of millstones and the people of his house
and took his belongings and the belongings of Yazdayard, and
fetched him out (made him to go out) from the Murghab. Then
they put (made) him in a coffin of (from) wood. Then some of
them assert that they carried him to Persepolis, then he was
buried in it on the first of the year 31.

TABARI.

48. The Finding of the Cross.

And in the two and twentieth year from the reign of
Constantine, there travelled his mother Hilani unto Jerusalem
and built in it churches for the Christians. Then Makariyus the
bishop pointed her upon the place of the Cross, then she dug it,
then, lo, a grave and three pieces of wood. They assert that
they did not know the Cross sought from the three pieces of
wood except by (the fact) that she placed every one of (from)
them upon a dead person who had become wasted away, then he
arose alive when she put upon him a piece of wood from them.
Then they made (worked) on account of that a feast, it was
known among them by 'the feast of the Cross.' And Hilani
worked for it a casing of (from) gold, and built the Church of the
Resurrection. And she appointed Makariyus over the remainder
of the Church. And the space of what was between the birth of
Christ and the appearing of the Cross was three hundred and
eight and twenty years.

MAKRĪZI.

49. THE SWORD AND THE PEN.

Know that the sword and the pen are both (each) of them an instrument to the master of the dynasty by which he asks for assistance upon his affair. Except that the need for (unto) the sword in beginning (first) of the dynasty, as long as its people [are engaged] in the setting in order (smoothing) of their affair is greater (more violent) than the need for the pen. Seeing that the pen in that state is a servant only, transmitting (carrying out) the Sultanic decision. And like that (is it) in the end of the dynasty when (since) its solidarity is weak and its people few for what overtakes (acquires) them of (the) decrepitude. And as to in the midmost of the dynasty, the master of it is able to dispense with the sword to a certain extent (some of the thing from the sword), because he—his affair has become smooth, his care (anxiety) does not remain except in the gathering (making to result) of the fruits of the reign (consisting) of the tax and the keeping order and the carrying through of the decisions. And the pen—it is the (one) assisting him in that; then is mighty the need to make it creak, and the swords will be laid aside in the sleeping places of their scabbards.

IBN KHALDŪN.

50. THE RARITIES OF BUZURJUMIHR, THE SAGE[1] OF THE PERSIANS.

He said : The counsellors have counselled me and the exhorters have exhorted me with anxiousness and counsel and educating : then no one exhorted me like my own gray hairs, nor did there counsel me the like of my own thought. I owned freemen and slaves, but none owned me nor overcome me save my own passion. I sought rest for my soul and found nothing more restful to it than its leaving alone what concerns it not. I have ridden the seas and seen the terrors, then I saw no terror like

[1] wise.

standing [still] by the door of an oppressive Sultan. I have roughed it in the wilds and the mountains, yet never saw a more savage than an evil mate[1]. I have eaten bitter herbs and drunk myrrh, then did not see ought more bitter than poverty. I have wrought[2] iron and transported rock, then saw no burden heavier than debt. I have been detained long in[3] prison, and fastened in fetters and beaten with rods[4] of iron, but nothing pulled me down as grief and care and sorrow pulled me down. I sought riches for their own sake[5] : then have not seen a richer than the content. I have given alms with treasures, then have not seen an alms more useful than turning back of the owner of an error to guidance. I have seen isolation and exile and the state of abasement, then did not see a more abasing thing than the harsh conduct of the evil neighbour[6]. I have mortared up the edifice in order to attain greatness by it and to be remembered, then saw no honour more elevated than the performance of kindness. I have worn splendid clothes, then never wore anything like goodness[7]. I have sought the best of things in the opinion of men, then have not found a thing better than beauty of character.

TURTŪSHI.

[1] the mate of evil.   [2] treated.   [3] my life has been prolonged to.   [4] tent-poles.   [5] from their own respects.   [6] the neighbour the evil (badness).   [7] soundness.

PART III

EASIER NEWSPAPER EXTRACTS

1. "BETWEEN THE INKHORNS AND THE LEAVES."

The readers will see in that which I make to go down under this title a sudden leaping (transporting of itself) sometimes (at one of the times) from (one) subject to another. And the reason in this is that I do not find these bewildering particles upon one page or in one book, but I am, as say the English, ' a worm of books.' I read much, then I stumble upon one (thing) here and one there, between newspaper and magazine and book. So I collect them under this title, as follows (like what comes) :

2. THE CROSS HAFIZ.

It was said to one of the Koran-reciters once, ' Read to us the chapter of Mary, for in the mosque is one of the Christians, and they love to hear it.' Then the Koran-reciter became cross and began muttering and saying : ' We will not read anything for the pleasure of the Christians.'

3. THE BULL-FIGHT. I.

And after that a door was opened in the circle of the playground and there came on the scene from it a bull into the open of the arena ornamented upon its back with ribbons of different colours. And it began going round in the circle with violent haste. Then the toreadors[1] came within reach of it. Then it made to butt one of them with its rough horns : then he escaped from it and put himself in possession of flight. And it was, as often as it got near them, they would frighten it by waving at it with large pieces of red stuff, then it would butt the air with its horns. Then it would move round and round them. Then they would not delay that they should return to the attack upon it. So now they would be exciting it, and now pelting it with darts between its shoulders ; and as often as they escaped from it there would pour itself out upon them the clapping from every place, and the folk would cheer in approval with a cheering almost deafening the ears.

4. The Bull-fight. II.

And lastly the bull would be scared and uncover its canine tooth, and its eyes would grow red from rage and the volcano of its anger would break out. Then it would not see an access to the curing of its thirst for revenge except the poor horse on which one of the toreadors rode[2]. Then it would rush upon it with violence and rip up its belly, and as for its rider, he would find to safety a path.

Few among those present are those who are moved[3] by this horrible spectacle ! And if you say to them this is a savage custom which ought to be abolished[4], they will become scared at you and look at you askance, and say, Nay on the contrary it must continue[5] because it trains in the soul the habit of courage, and teaches the man venturesomeness and horsemanship. And how many a custom which is approved with a folk is disapproved in the opinion of others. ' And to God in regard to His creation are businesses.'

[1] wrestlers.   [2] the riding upon it one, etc.   [3] impressed.
[4] its abolishing is necessary.   [5] the making it remain is necessary.

5. THE NEW POETRY.

Poetry—the register of the Arabs—the Ignorance and the first Islamic ages were raising up its renown and glorifying the maker of it. Afterwards its shadow shrank in the last ages. Then there did not originate in it save individuals who imitated the ancients and did not attain their attainment. In the bloom of the Abbasid dynasty Irak was the mine of poetry. Then when the misfortunes came one behind the other upon it its vestige was erased or it slept long and only waked up from its nap in our own age. And there have emerged in it great poets, and the most of them in the valley of the Nile. They have broken the bonds of imitation and have strung it in a new fashion, upon which is the brilliance of the settled country and the virility of the nomad life. And this renaissance is, by my life, the first-fruits of abundant education. The time will not be long until its fruit will be much and it will come with the wonderful which was not in the reckoning.

6. POETRY AND PROSE.

Poetry is distinguished from prose by metre and it, on account of its being set to music, is light upon the brain and the intellect is brisk to the hearing of it, and the good spirit finds pleasure in it. Then when its expression is good and contains a meaning worth mention, such as attaining wisdom or chiding exhortation or fresh description or pitiful tale and so on, the pleasure of the intellect is doubled by it, and it keeps alive afterwards the maker of it as long as[1] God wills. Then it pleases every one who hears it or reads it in thousands of the years. And no wonder, for it is of the beautiful handicrafts, which much of humanity[2] have not ceased glorifying of old and of late ; and it will remain glorious as long as the intellect remains. Then the maker of it becomes great and is reckoned of the mighty, and his name is perpetuated in the bellies of the journals and the mouths of men.

[1] to what.　　[2] the flesh.

7. The Essence of Poetry.

We say that poetry is distinguished from prose by metre; and it is that which makes it difficult. And that is natural. It is not possible that we should obviate it. Only that to poetry amongst us is another difficulty which is not less than the difficulty of the metre and it is the obligatoriness of the accord in the rhyming consonant to which the poet is forced, that he should build the end of every verse of his ode, be it[1] short or long, upon one letter homogeneous of the vowel and of the *sukūn*, and similarly the vowel and *sukūn* of what is before it. And this is not in reality a part of poetry at all[2]. Is not the one verse which we recite poetry in all of its meaning although we do not recite to it a second, in which the listener may be sensible of the accord of the rhyming consonant? And perhaps the reciter of it was not remembering its second: or that it was a single one in itself, the maker of it not having articulated with other than it. Then do you opine that that singleness lowers its poetic value?

8. The Poetry of the Future.

Indeed let the poets know that this facilitation of Poetry is inevitable: there is no escape from it. Then if it be not completed in this our day upon our tongue it will be completed to-morrow upon the tongue of other than us from the poets of the future. Then at that time the honour of it will have passed us by. And, verily, I indeed opine that it is timely in this our age— the age of progress—that we should untie the tether of imitation and go cheerfully to the work with a freedom which will insure to us success, so that we may bring the poetry of the future near to the present.

[1] were it. [2] And this is not in the truth from the poetry in a thing.

9. BLANK-VERSE[1].

Those who are informed about the literatures of the western languages say that of their poets are those who do not necessitate to themselves sometimes the accord of the rhyming consonant in their poetry. And this form of the poetry is spreading among them with the spreading of other than it. Then if their saying be correct, then I seek that this form of the poetry be found amongst us also like other than it, and we shall name it the Neglected to distinguish it from the poetry bound by the rhyming consonant, and I do not seek that it should render vain the old form completely.

10. THE HIGH DOWLAH[2] AND GERMANY.

They say that what instigates the Germans upon making for the Ottoman countries is that they see the countries of the East to be fertile of herbages, in which nature works more than man, overflowing with the raw materials, and there is no handicraft in them. For that, they come with what is necessary to them of the instruments and the implements, for the manufacturing of which there is requisite troublesome work and business connections[3]. So the lords of cleverness of the Europeans find in the East two benefits doubled. Then they return to the Ottoman countries of the wares more than what they take from them of the raw materials, and that is because the wares which come from England or France are of good quality, but they are dear in price.

11. THE COMPLAINT OF THE EGYPTIAN WIFE.

My father died as you know and bequeathed to me property of which I put my husband in possession. Then he squandered it in wine and gaming. Then I had winked at his slips out of pity and compassion for him until, when my hand was empty and my pasture had become desert, I perceived from him *ennui*,

[1] See below.   [2] Dynasty.   [3] interconnected.

which was inviting him to the evil of my companionship, and he was oftentimes jeering at me and saying: Verily I do not love the ignorant woman who does not understand me nor I her, and at times he was hinting at me and saying : Verily the happy man is he who is blessed with a learned wife who will read to him the newspapers and the novels, and who will discuss with him about the political and intellectual questions. Nay, he was passing on from the hinting to the plain speaking. Then he would say as often as he entered upon me, saying Uff, Uff! grumbling : O that I had a wife who makes good the dancing and the singing and the beating upon the piano !

12. THE (WOMEN) ARBITRATORS.

A judge once elected twelve women for the hearing of one of the lawsuits and the decision in regard to it. Then when they had secluded themselves in the room of the conferring for the looking into the decision, one of them offered an opinion in regard to an affair other than the lawsuit. Then the remaining ones wheeled round to the inquiring in regard to it and forgot what they had been summoned unto ; and the judge awaiting their decision was forced by the becoming exhausted of patience unto the dismissing them with (a) peace and to repeat the lawsuit before arbitrators (consisting) of the men. And thus will be the state of the woman in every affair when she leaves alone the management of the house and the children and takes to the management of men and countries[1].

13. THE HIJAZ RAILWAY.

And all the works of the line indicate perfect cleverness in the engineering and accuracy in the work and mighty patience in enduring the troubles in the cutting of the towering mountains and originating the high bridges over the many valleys. And the excellence—all the excellence—in that belongs to the Otto-

[1] the worshippers and the country.

man engineers (and they were 34 engineers); Yes, verily the greatest chief engineer over them is a German, but he was not the whole of the intellect managing the work. Nay, verily the Ottoman engineers both[1] civil and military were partners with him in the work up to the station of Al-Ala. And they have been by themselves[2] in the work, all of it, from Al-Ala to Medina, since none but Muslims are permitted to enter[3] the land of the Hijaz, which makes its beginning from this point or from Medain Salih[4], a station before it[5].

And to the line belong 72 locomotives[6], 12 first class coaches upholstered in the best style[7], and 30 third class passenger coaches, and along[9] the line are 32 steam instruments for pumping[10] the water from the wells.

14. THE COMFORT OF THE PASSENGERS.

When it was the hour one and a half after the noon, the train moved: but before it moved the brigadier Kazim Pasha passed over the whole of the passengers who had been invited, inquiring about[11] their places and their comfort, asking each man about what it was necessary that he should be accompanied (with) in his compartment, in order that he might unite two (persons) acquainted with one another in their sittings, for there had been given to every two a compartment of the compartments of the train, in order that each side of it might be a couch for a person to sleep on.

15. THE HIJAZ TRAIN.

And the carriages which were on this train are the most splendid of what are on the Hijaz railway, not having been ridden in before this time, upholstered[12] in fine wax-cloth with taste[13],

[1] of. [2] single. [3] for want of permission of entering of other than the Muslim. [4] the cities of Salih. [5] before it by a station. [6] engines. [7] carriages from mistresses of the first degree carpeted with the best carpeting. [8] carriages of riding. [9] in. [10] making to go out. [11] reviewing. [12] carpeted. [13] arrangement.

and gilded with the best gilding, and painted with the best
painting, and vaulted of the roof, like the carriages of the *train-
de-luxe* in Egypt, except that it was more in firmness and more
solid in building. And in every carriage was a place for washing
the face and hands or for the ablution, and the water was always
plentiful in it. And in the train is a long carriage in which are
chairs of straw and bamboo in its sides, to be used[1] as an
apartment for sitting—'Saloon'—and it was in two divisions,
so that[2], if some of the passengers wanted not to be with some
others, they took to themselves one of the divisions. And in it
also is a carriage set apart[3] for the obtaining of food[4], and three
carriages for the necessary things of the food of kitchen and
cellar, containing[5] all that the epicure seeks in his alightingplace.
And there are servants who are looking after the service with the
best looking after ; so they make the fruits and greens and snow
of Syria last[6] to Medina, and some of the fruits of Medina to
Syria.

16. FROM DAMASCUS TO AL-KISWAH.

We left the Hotel Victoria in which we had alighted in
Damascus (and it is the largest hotel in this city) when it was
the fifth hour Arabic, and the eleventh and a half before the noon
on the European counting. We made for the station of Al-Kadam
al-Sherif which is south of the city and is distant from the heart
of the city where we were by about 40 minutes by the travelling
of the carriages. And in front of this little station are storehouses and repairing shops[7], elevated of building, solid, sufficient
for the businesses of the line from the direction of Damascus,
because the largest storehouses have been erected[8] by the side of
Edrei, as will be mentioned below[9].

[1] for its being taken to oneself. [2] until. [3] particularized.
[4] acquiring for oneself the food. [5] assembling. [6] preserve carefully
the fruits, etc. [7] magazines for the repair. [8] originated.
[9] as its clearing up will come.

Then when it was the hour one and a half after the noon the train moved. This train travelled cutting steppes and deserts, and we were seeing, after it had been absent from us, a view of Jilliq[1] the Extensive, after trees here and there, to the station of Al-Kiswah at a distance of 20 kilometres from it. Rarely were we seeing the trees and shrubs after that, except that most of the land which we passed over to about 200 kilometres was good[2] for agriculture, and that the bulk of it had been sown[3] with[4] wheat and chick-peas and barley and maize, and was reaped.

17. EDREI.

The engineers have divided the line into four divisions, and have placed for it distinct maps, in which are the names of the stations and their distances and the altitudes[5] of the places above sea level[6], and others showing the places of the Arab tribes upon the two sides[7] of the line.

Then the first division—they make it from Al-Kadam al-Sherif to Maan where is the kilometre 460. And this division is accepting cultivation, until it is like the land of Syria itself. And included in[8] this division is the station of Edrei, which is[9] the junction for the two lines from Haifa and from Damascus. And at this junction rise the lofty buildings and storehouses for the repair of the locomotives and carriages which some damage has befallen[10], and the largest magazines for the storing of the trains and carriages upon necessity. And there are erected at it a large refectory and hospital and shops for the sellers and *cafés*. And as to this large plain there are placed in it heaps of grain[11], which are weighed by the thousands of quarters : between some of them lie the sacks full of produce, one above another like city walls, for barriers[12] between the neighbours—of what indicates

[1] (a poetical name of Damascus, fem.).　　[2] sound.　　[3] pc.　　[4] acc.
[5] elevations.　　[6] from the surface of the water.　　[7] directions.
[8] And of the sum of.　　[9] has taken to itself.　　[10] hit.　　[11] mounds of the crops.　　[12] limits.

increase of security and goodness of protection between men. And as to Edrei itself it is a town in which are about 1000 houses[1] or about 5000 souls, and it is distant from the station about half-an-hour to the foot passenger, and before long[2] Edrei the station will become a new city to which will transport themselves the people of the ancient city, or they will become dependent upon it[3] for the necessary things of livelihood and life.

18. Dhat al Hajj.

And as to the second division, it is from Maan to Tabuk. And this division comprises of the famous places Dhat al Hajj at kilometre 610. And in it is a large fortress, the duty of which before the construction[4] of the railway was to guard[5] the Sultanic route at a point which was famous for the raids[6] of the (nomadic) Arabs and particularly those who were time after time using deceit to stop up the large spring which is there, because the Arabs were putting themselves in possession by that anciently of the cutting of the road upon the pilgrims through thirst, and of spoiling and plundering them, after that their strengths were failing, or they were perishing. So a number[7] of fortresses were built on the route to guard[5] the springs, so that the raiders[8] should not choke them with earth.

19. The Country near Maan.

And between the Castle and Maan the lands are found flat, accepting agriculture, but what is sown of them is very little by the side of what is not sown, for the scarcity[9] of water or for the want of managing the water of the rains which alights on them.

And as to after Maan to Medina, little is there found in it land good[10] for agriculture, except narrow valleys between lofty

---

[1] alightingplaces.   [2] it will not be distant that.   [3] followers
to it.   [4] origination.   [5] preserve.   [6] treacheries.   [7] sum
[8] traitors.   [9] fewness.   [10] sound.

mountains which the scour has made (into) trenches : then there
grow upon the sides of its flow wormwood and thorn and some
trees and shrubs, the greenness of which indicates that their
places (are) fit for cultivation[1], if the waters of the scours were
managed in them ; and the management of them will be by
originating treasuries and tanks for them, as the people of
Lebanon do in the heights in which there are no springs.

The Bedawin have begun in some of the places getting near
with their tents to[2] the stations on account of their perceiving
their being benefited from them. But all that is in the first half
of the line, from the direction of Syria. As to the second half
of it towards Medina, and particularly from the station of Al-
Hadyah and what is adjacent to it southwards, then verily it is
other than accepting colonization upon the sides of the line, but
upon a distance from it the Arabs dwell in their tents, and they
are not dwelling except where are found herbage and water.

20. AL-ALA.

As to the southern division of the line, there is not in it of
the flourishing green except Al-Ala, where is the kilometre 980
from Damascus, and except Al-Akhdar where is the kilometre
760 ; and the first is more of green, and the second is more
abundant and palatable of water. So in Al-Ala are found
plantations of palm grove and fruit trees[3], of the deepest green[4], or
it is the rather between the colours, because its green is shining,
inclining to the blackness.

On our return we passed over Al-Ala by night. And it was
of the goodness of the management that the passing upon the
stations was made on the return journey the opposite of what it
was[5] on the outward journey, until we were obtaining a sight[6] of

[1] accepting the growing (tr.).   [2] from.   [3] trees of the fruits.
[4] with the most violent of what exists, in respect of greenness (acc.).   [5] the
opposite of it.   [6] putting ourselves in possession of a vision.

most of the landmarks of the line and views of the wildernesses
and mountains.

And as to the station of Al-Akhdar, its trees are few, but the
hand of man has started propagation from them, and a (long)
time will not pass away, until this district will be a mistress of
fruits and flowers.

21. TABUK.

Tabuk is a small town, mistress of palms and vines and fruits,
at the kilometre 692. And it is the city famous for one of the
raids of the Prophet (God pray over him and salute !). And
thirst had become violent in it upon his companions (the
acceptance of God upon them !). Then was what is famous in
the Biography of the gushing of water from between his fingers
abundantly, until he quenched the thirst of them all. And one
of pious[1] ancestry had taken to himself at this place a mosque
which had fallen into ruin through length of time; but his
governmentship Kazim Pasha renewed it at the command of the
excellency of the most mighty Sultan. And the well from which
the water gushed in the time of the Prophet (God pray over him
and salute !) does not cease (being) preserved, attended to,
reckoned of the greatest of the relics[2] of the Apostleship[3] and its
bright miracles. And it is now in the areas of the mosque upon
the right of one entering it[4]. Between it and the door are about
four metres. We drank from it on our return from the journey
(because we on our outward journey to Medina the Ennobled
passed it by night) and we prayed in the mosque the midday
prayer. And it is a little mosque, only that it is fair to see[5], the
likest thing to the cell which the late Sheikh Jemal ed Din
Efendi, kadi of Egypt, erected[6] formerly[7] in the neighbourhood[8] of
his dwelling[9] in Kasr ed Dubarah—only that this mosque, has a
pulpit, in which the Friday prayers are said[10] and the common

[1] sound.　　[2] traces.　　[3] Mission.　　[4] its enterer.　　[5] beautiful of
view.　　[6] originated.　　[7] previously.　　[8] protection.　　[9] alighting
place.　　[10] the Friday is prayed.

prayer constituted. And it is standing[1] at the extremity of the town, from what is adjacent to the station westwards ; and the distance between it [the mosque] and it [the station] is about 25 minutes.

22. MADA'IN SALIH[2].

The third division is from Tabuk to Al-Badai', and in this division is Al-Ala, the description of which has preceded, and Mada'in Salih, and it is at kilometre 955. And it is the Mada'in the eclipsing of which with its people is mentioned in the noble Koran. And perchance it was eclipsed by a fiery volcano, like what results now often in known directions of the earth. And that which appears of the views of these cities now is mountains, in which the scours and the sun have wrought with the mightiest of doings. So you see pieces from the mountains towering up, which have been split and separated (some) from others of them and their forms vary. Then some of them have risen like the high building, beneath which[3] the caves, natural or hewn by the act of an agent, appear as if they were doors, with their props turned upside down, their bases having become their lintels[4]. And the best of what is said in describing it is what his honour[5] the excellent Mohammad Bey al-Muweilihi said— " Verily they are nature's antiques." And we do not think that there are found any mountains like[6] the mountains of Mada'in Salih, which bewilder the spectator[7], and point to[8] ancientness of time, of which none knows the beginning[9] except the Creator (great and glorious is He!). And upon what mountains do the scours descend[10] with the force[11] with which they descend[10] upon these mountains? And what sun almost kindles the stone with fire like the sun of the Hijaz ?

Such we saw Mada'in Salih and much of the mountains which adjoin it southwards to Medina.

[1] falling. [2] The cities of Salih. [3] in the lowest part of them.
[4] their low has been made their high. [5] presence. [6] in the appear-
ances of. [7] one seeing. [8] indicate. [9] the first. [10] alight.
[11] in the amount.

23. The Arabs and the Hijaz Railway.

Some of these tribes especially those near to Medina the
Illumined are mischief making, disliking the construction of the
iron line because they see it divesting (them of) their being
benefited from their camels upon which they carry all the visitors
of Medina and the pilgrims of the House, and all the foodstuffs
and merchandise.   And Medina was, two months of time ago
threatened by their raids ; and accordingly soldiers were placed
upon the summits of the mountains and the mouths of the roads
upon the two sides of the line from Mada'in Salih to Medina the
Illumined.   And we had, as soon as we got near to Medina the
Illumined, seen the great numbers[1] of the soldiers.   Their tents
and entrenchments were scattered over the summits of the
mountains and main roads of the valleys.   And the number of the
soldiers[2] now guarding[3] between Medina and Mada'in Salih
amounts to 15,000 soldiers : of them in Medina alone about
8,000 and the rest[4] upon the two sides of the line from it
northwards.

24. Antar's Stable.

The fourth division is from Al-Badai', which is at kilometre
1000, to Medina the Illumined, at which kilometre 1303 comes
to an end ; and that is the amount of the distance which is
between it and Damascus.   And as to the line between Haifa
and Medina the Ennobled, it is 1480 kilometres.   And of the
spots famed in this division is the Stable of Antar at kilometre
1190 ; and it is a building elevated upon the summit of a high
mountain, which looks towards the station of Al-Buwair as if
it were in the neighbourhood of it[5].   And Al-Buwair is at
kilometre 1210, and it is famous for its water.   And there is not
in this division a place possessed of abundant water, good to
drink[6] except this place.

[1] the muchness.   [2] armies.   [3] preserving carefully.   [4] remaining
ones.   [5] nearness from it.   [6] sound for the drinking.

And perchance the readers will be content with this account[1]
of the Hamidian Line; by means of which we arrived from
Damascus to Medina the Illumined in the space of three days, of
which about 27 hours were for the performance[2] of the prayers
and the obtaining[3] of food. And this our journey was accomplished with all the means[4] of comfort and pleasantness, were it
not for the violence[5] of the tread of the heat upon us between
Al-Badai' and Medina the Illumined (upon whose Inhabitant be
the most excellent prayer and peace) since it was there 44
degrees on our outward journey, and it reached[6] on our return
journey 48.

25. ADVANTAGES OF THE HIJAZ RAILWAY.

He who passes over many[7] of the stations of the province of
Al-Karak will find heaps of wheat and chick-peas and barley (in)
great mounds some beside others of them, belonging to the
merchants who have pitched their tents by the side of them,
waiting for transport wagons[8] on which to transport these foodstuffs to Damascus and Haifa; as he will find many[7] of the
wagons[8] loaded waiting for the engines to travel with them; and
as he will find caravans of camels coming to some of them, being
reckoned by the hundreds, train after train, and before each one
of them a banner spread abroad, white or red or stamped in
allusion to the master of the caravan from (among) the merchants;
and they have come in from Hauran or from the open valley of
As-Salt to those stations for that end. And the products of
these districts were, before the erection[9] of the railway, being left
alone where they stood[10] usually, because their transporting upon
camels upon distances which are counted by days and weeks was
making their expenses double their price. Whereas now[11] they
are being transported upon a journey of ten or twenty or thirty

---

[1] clearing up.　　[2] paying.　　[3] acquiring for ourselves.　　[4] causes.
[5] the becoming violent.　　[6] arrived at.　　[7] much.　　[8] carriages.
[9] originating.　　[10] in their (its) places.　　[11] As to now.

hours at the most at a charge[1] varying from a dollar to a half for a quarter, and its price where it stands[2] varies between 60 and 70 piastres. Then it will arrive at the station of Edrei, for example, for 70 or 80 piastres. So the merchant will find from it if he exports it to Syria or Haifa a profit, after that the sower was finding from it lost capital[3].

26. The Deposed Pasha.

We stopped in the station of Al-Ala about an hour of time, because the deposed guardian[4] of Medina was stopping in it; and we were on our outward journey to Medina, whereas[5] he was on his return journey towards Damascus. So he transported himself from his carriage, in which he was with his family, to our train, and he sat with us in the saloon talking together with the brigadier and the commandant. And the grief was visible upon his face, for he was anticipating[6] after his deposition evil. His condition was lamentable[7]; because he was placed in a carriage from the second class[8], in which there are no chairs nor seats; and he had carpeted it and made to its windows blinds, that it might be suitable for his relatives and his family to sleep in comfort in it. But the like of these carriages are the most violent of what is, upon the traveller in both heat and cold for injury; because they are other than firm of make: there is not upon their windows glass—and we will speak[9] about this man in another place.

27. The Representation of Damascus.

The city of Damascus of Syria has been directed (by God) to select a man excellent, well-informed, faithful in his love of his government and nation who will be made a candidate to represent

---

[1] hire.   [2] in their (its) places.   [3] head of money which was going the ways of the winds.   [4] preserving carefully.   [5] and.
[6] thinking there would befall.   [7] what an elegy is composed for.   [8] degree.
[9] the speech will come.

it in the assembly[1] of those sent—namely[2], his honour[3] the excellent Azm-Zadeh resident of Egypt from some time, and known among us for his education and gentleness and excellence. And I interviewed him in reference to the affair of this candidature of his, to the following effect[4] :—

I said: What will be your programme when you sit to represent Damascus ?

He said : If I am elected member of the Ottoman parliament for Damascus and Al-Karak—and they are the provinces for which I make myself[5] a candidate—my programme will be to serve the country.

28. ECHO OF THE FREEDOM IN INDIA.

Scarcely had the telegraphic news arrived at the districts of India informing of the granting by His Excellency the Sultan to his nation Freedom, when[6] the Indian newspapers began publishing the good tidings and leading out articles of praise and panegyric regarding the Commander of the Believers and his loved nation. Then the spirits revived and the Muslims exchanged mutual congratulations, and told mutual good tidings of success and prosperity. And God has verified the saying of his prophet— on whom be prayer and peace—where he said, My nation are like the building, one part of it firmly binding another.

29. THE POLITICIAN.

Oftentimes the slayer slays, then when he is done with his affair he sits by the side of his slain weeping over him with the weeping of bereaved (mother) over her unique (one). Oftentimes the stealer steals, then when he has finished his requirement he raises up his hand supplicating unto God that He may provide him the money lawfully, until he will not acquire it for himself unlawfully. As to the politician, then he does not see a day in

---

[1] sitting.   [2] he (is).   [3] the presence of.   [4] as comes.   [5] my soul.
[6] except and.

his life happier than the day in which he knows that he—there
has been perfect to him his management in the causing to perish
of a community or the reducing to poverty of a nation. And
the sign of that (is) that he in the day of his triumph as he
names it, he—or the day of his crime as I name it, I—he hears
the outcry of those who make outcry, comfortable of (the) heart,
frigid of (the) breast, and it is fancied to him that the open
(ground) in his earth and his sky is more narrow than that it
should have capacity for his heart, flying, soaring with joy and
gladness.

30. WINE IN EGYPT. I.

There is nothing which pains the Muslim zealous for his
religion like that he should see his brethren the Muslims dispersed
in the taverns and by-paths of the ways imbibing the poisons of
intoxicants without that there seize them scruple or caring, as if
they were drinking the declared lawful of the drink. And of the
wonderful is that a writer will write an article and publish it
in the newspapers in which he investigates[1] with religious
investigation—perhaps contradicts in it what is famous and
handed down in the opinion of men of religion—then these will
spring upon[2] him with an inauspicious spring and unsheathe out
of the seeking of revenge swords with which they wrest the
sentence against him, whilst they see morning and evening the
masses[3] of the Muslims, nay the pick[4] of them, drinking the
intoxicants openly[5]. And there does not seize them religious
zeal instigating them upon the formation[6] of a society from them,
which should work for the lessening of the evil of the intoxicants
and the putting away[7] of the temptation of them from the
Muslims.

[1] scrapes.   [2] rebel against.   [3] commonalty.   [4] particularity.
[5] in public.   [6] composition.   [7] pushing.

31. Wine in Egypt. II.

No religion interdicts wine as[1] the Mohammadan religion interdicted it. And no community is addicted to the being devoted to it with excess and greed[2] like the Egyptians. And no government has neglected the affair of its subjects and winked at them devoting themselves to the poisons, until it is as if they were wishing their rooting out, like the Egyptian government. And no men of religion have fallen short in their duty, which Divine providence entrusted to them, like the learned of the Muslims. And their falling short is in combating the likes of this evil and forestalling the commonalty before that the wines and their poisons and the being accustomed upon them carry them away.

And verily we see the government taking pains with the warding off of the plagues and lavishing the whole hundredweights of the money in the path of guarding from them, and not considering about lessening the evil of the wines. If it were not for keeping[3] (about) the health of its community, then let it be for the sake of copying the rest of the civilized governments, which do not cease endeavouring in narrowing the circle of the evils of those poisons. And perhaps the winking of the government at this matter was the greatest incitement to the commonalty in being devoted to the intoxicants.

32. The Peninsula of Arabia[4].

In the Peninsula is the Kiblah of the Muslims altogether. There turn towards it every day three hundred millions at the least at the five times [of prayer]. There is no difference between Indian and Egyptian and Turk and Chinaman.

The Peninsula—in it is the grave of the Master of the Message and the place of descent of the Revelation, and in it are

---

[1] with the like of what.   [2] gluttony.   [3] acc.
[4] The Island of the Arabs.

ten millions of the sons of those Arabs who spread abroad Islam and waged a holy war in exalting the word of the Religion. And they are now in a state—the face of humanity becomes black at[1] the mention of it.

33. Religious Significance of Arabia.

Then if you direct to the Indian or other than him these questions, for example, 'Whence comes to you this religion which you profess?' he says, 'From the Arabs.' 'In what tongue is your heavenly book, and in what place was it sent down?' he says, 'In the tongue of the Arabs, and in the Island of the Arabs.' 'Where do you turn your face when you wish the communion with[2] your Lord in the state of your stress[3] and difficulty?' he answers you, 'The country of the Arabs.' 'Which direction is the Kiblah? In which tongue do you address Him in the state of your supplication and prayer?' 'In the tongue of the Arabs.' 'Where is the resting-place of your Prophet and the place of his relics and the rites of your religion?' 'In the country of the Arabs.' 'Who are the preservers of the tongue of the perspicuous Book?' 'They are the Arabs.' So the Arabs and their country are the root of the religion. If they be sound and the state[4] of their country be sound, the religion is sound. And every one who relates himself to this faith [it is well], and if not then the reverse without a doubt.

34. The Decadence of Al-Islam.

For this we see the Indian crying out and screaming upon his folk (that), 'Arise and bestir yourselves and look at your brothers in Russia.' And the Chinaman ascends the pulpit and incites his clan to wake up[5], and that they should shoe themselves with

---

[1] from.   [2] of.   [3] harm.   [4] state of things.
[5] upon the awaking.

the shoeing of their brothers the Indians. And the Iranian writes to his nation (that), 'Resemble the people of Egypt.' And the Moor stamps in his blood (saying), 'Imitate your brothers the Turks.' And the Turk mutters to his party : 'Verily, we will imitate the Egyptian.'

And verily our condition is to be[1] grieved for to the (full) extent[2] of what we see and hear of the yearning and the sighing and the heaving of the sighs and the lamenting of the condition from all the extremities of the Islamic world. And each points to him who is more remote than himself in the districts ; and the whole are agreeing that the state of things universal to the Islamic world is evil.

35. THE NEEDS OF ARABIA.

It is the duty of[3] the Islamic nation in[4] this state of things— and especially the Egyptian—to direct its looks to the Peninsula and equip it with a part[5] of its arts and sciences and its professors, and to spread abroad amongst its people the banners[6] of science and culture as are spread abroad amongst us the juridical sciences and other than they. And the greatest surety to us for the continuance of these[7] is the Azhar Mosque even if it were demanding much of the reforming.

36. THE LIGHTING OF THE MEDINA MOSQUE.

The number of the Aghas of the Haram is forty Aghas, and they are taking in hand the service of the noble chamber ; and of their duty is that they should let down the lamps of the mosque with a grapnel of which the head is of iron, in order that the kindlers may light them. And they are of the chamberlains of the Haram, and the number of these chamberlains is 560 chamberlains. But they, on account of their number,[8] take in

---

[1] will be. [2] end. [3] The necessary upon. [4] and.
[5] division. [6] flags. [7] upon their continuance. [8] muchness.

turns the service as to sweeping[1] and carpeting and trimming of
the lamps and lighting them. And the operation of the lamps
upon them has become light now, because the noble mosque is
lighted by electricity now, so there are not lighted of the lamps
most of them.

37. THE AMERICAN TRAIN.

(By[2] our excellent special correspondent in New York.)

Important businesses determined upon me the journey to
this city. Then I came to it upon a train—there suffices in
describing it that it be said that it is of the recent American
design[3]. In it are couches for the sleeping and a feeding-place
for the eating, extreme in the arrangement and the good quality
of the eatables, and a library, in it much of the books and the
newspapers and the magazines, and a charming saloon for sitting,
the man does not feel with it a thing of the weariness of the
journey or boredom and ill humour. And there also is a barber's
shop, I tried therein the cleansing of my beard from the hair for
the first time. Then I was bewildered at the pre-eminence of
the hairdresser in qualifying the motions of the razor upon the
motions of the train in order that he might not shed innocent
blood. And in that train is a box for the mail in which the
passengers place their despatches, the administration of the post
emptying it at every station.

38. THE PRESERVING OF THE NATURAL RESOURCES.

(By the[4] special correspondent of the *Muaiyad*.)

The president of the Republic is famed for being[5] an inventor
not an imitator, even if all of what he sets about or endeavours
after[6] the perfecting of is strange and new and bewildering.

[1] acc. [2] By the presence of. [3] fashion. [4] the presence of the.
[5] in that he is. [6] unto.

Now he has assembled in these days the governors of the American states all of them in Washington the capital to hold[1] a congress to inquire into the means[2] available to the guarding of the natural resources of the country, such as the different mines and the forests, and the being sparing in the spending from them, preserving[3] what remains for the needs of the country in the future centuries. And he has permitted to each one of them that he should take with him as companions three men from the people of science and true experience in the matters for the sake of which the congress was held[4].

39. THE HOUSE[5] OF AL-ARQAM.

[It is a dwelling in Mecca the Honoured to which the Prophet (whom may God pray over and salute) used to resort, and those of the Companions who became Moslems before the appearing of their affair, used to study the Koran together in it.]

Of the places by the visitation of which one wins a blessing in Mecca the Honoured for their association[6] with the history of the first inception of Islam is the dwelling known by 'the dwelling of Al-Arqam'; or 'the dwelling of Al-Khaizuran'; and this is the dwelling standing[7] in one of the slopings near to Al-Safa. Its appearance is not of what arrests the look, seeing that there is not to it save one face—it is the Kiblah one—of which the measurement scarcely exceeds four metres.

40. THE COURTYARD.

And over the door of this dwelling the looker sees an Arabic inscription, about which we will speak below[8], and the door leads him who enters by[9] it into a small enclosure, upon its right hand a cupola little[10] of elevation resting upon columns tied to one

---

[1] knot. [2] accesses. [3] inf. [4] knotted. [5] dwelling.
[6] their being tied. [7] rising. [8] upon which the speech will come in what is after. [9] from. [10] few.

another by arches, two of which are blocked with light buildings.
And in the other direction of[1] the enclosure, face to face with
the cupola, is a small compartment, which was originally a
vestibule of[1] a small mosque, as appears from its blocked up
arches.

41. SEARCH FOR INSCRIPTIONS.

And when the visitation of this place takes place[2], there is
ordained along with it to the visitor a prayer of two bows of the
supererogatory things on account of the Prophet (whom may God
pray over and salute) finding shelter in it for a time at the
beginning of his sending.   Accordingly I set about the paying of
these two bows, and after that I directed my look to the walls of
the courtyard.   Perchance I might stumble upon an inscription
greater of value than the inscription of the door, I mean more
ancient than it in period.   Then I did not find it.

42. THE DISCOVERY.

Then I resolved upon the leaving, but whilst I was making[3]
ready to go out, I spied in one of the vaults of the cupola two
slabs of blue stone upon which was writing.   Then I reached out
to the first.   Then, lo, it was a piece, its length 58 centimetres,
and its breadth 28 centimetres, its writing in the Kufic script,
tree-shaped.   Its period goes back to the middle of the fifth
Hijrah century, as appears from the form of its letters and of its
embellishments.   And this inscription makes a beginning with
the ' Basmalah,' there is next to it the verse of ' In houses ' to His
saying (exalted be He) 'and in the evenings[4].'   Thereafter, ' This
is the hiding-place of the Apostle of God [break in the stone] and
his family, the dwelling of Al-Khaizuran.'

[1] from.   [2] was.   [3] pc.   [4] The whole verse is ' In houses which
God hath permitted to be raised, in which His name may be remembered, in
which men may praise Him in the mornings and in the evenings ': Koran,
24, 36.

And the second slab is of the blue stone likewise. Its length 85 centimetres and its breadth 40 centimetres. And in it are six lines in the Aiyūbī script of the *naskh*, and in it is an inscription too long to mention[1].

43. The Steamship "Sardinia."

Thousands of the men stopped upon the shore to witness the disaster of the steamship "Sardinia," and whilst she dashed herself on the rocks there shot out from her tongues of flame and smoke like what results in the volcanoes, and the warships had lost no time for the deliverance of the passengers with all care and energy, but the waves and the tumbling of the masts made their getting near to the steamship impossible; and for another reason[2], for the terrified Arabs renounced the leaping into the water and in an interval of ten minutes the steamship was surrounded by the flame, and some of her parts exploded and caused many[3] to perish; and the stokers and mechanics died in their compartments, since the line of retreat was cut upon them; and the engines[4] remained going round until the ship broke (her wing).

44. The Egyptian Newspapers.

I do not see the newspapers in Egypt (to be ought) save an assemblage of the assemblages of gambling, nor these writers (to be anything) but a company of the players, who have placed the heads of the Egyptians upon the table of the games as are placed the balls upon the billiard table. So they revolve round them playing with them and seeking to ward them off from each other. So in the morning Zaid gains them and 'Amr loses them in the evening, and perhaps the end of the night will not come until the ill-luck revolves its turn against them entirely: then the whole will lose them and the master of the assembly will gain them.

[1] its mention would be long.   [2] from another direction.   [3] much.
[4] instruments.

45. RELIGION AND PATRIOTISM.

Verily the impure patriotic sentiment has crept into the hearts of some men and chased the religious sentiment from its place and alighted in its alightingplace. And if it were the sound patriotism, it would indeed refuse that it should be like the serpent which has no burrow, so it extorts from every owner of a burrow his burrow and extrudes him from his habitation and abode. And the correct patriotism is a portion of religion, because religion commands the professor of religion, in what it commands him of good[1] works, that he should equip for the defence of[2] his homeland his equipment and that he should not make for its enemy to it a path. This is patriotism and this is its summary. He who has no good in regard to his religion has no good in regard to his homeland because he, if he were in his breaking the covenant of his patriotism a wicked traitor, then in his breaking the covenant of God and His contract, he is more treacherous and more wicked.

46. OF HISTORICAL TRUTH.

Then in the like of this state of things it behoves to us that we should uncover the cover from that truth in order that it may be revealed to our readers and to all of the lovers of the verification, that it is of the necessary in the like of those places that the historical truth should be above all of the sorts of the personal considerations[3]; and that there be not to the writer an object in view save the clearing up of the truth, and that he be not in any respect[4] making for making light of the ancient object of praise, or that he should praise himself, but that his main object[5] be to rehearse the facts according to what they are.

[1] sound.   [2] from.   [3] incitements.   [4] in a respect of the respects.
[5] the mass of his object.

47. THE OCCUPATION OF BOSNIA.

Next verily His Majesty[1] the Sultan sent a telegraphic message to Her Majesty[1] the Queen of England to conciliate her tender heart upon the peoples of Bosnia, and seeking from her the mediation with the government[2] of Austria in the preventing of the massacres and of the shedding of blood[3] by stopping the occupation until that the High Government[2] should be in a position to still the agitated thoughts and to content the peoples with the handing over and the acknowledging of the decision of the Powers. Then the Queen answered in a message gentle of purport showing[4] in it her grief for what was resulting of the shedding of blood, but saying in the end : ' Only that I see the means effectual to the making cease of this trouble and disorder— it is the subduing by the armies of Austria and the Hungarians of Herzegovina and Bosnia with a perfect subduing.'

48. THE BLOOD-WIT.

We mentioned in what has passed (away) the journey of the Damascus Mahmil from Mecca, and (now) there has come the news of its arrival at[5] Medina safely, and there did not happen to it on its way a thing which is worthy the mention save that a Bedawi man approached one of the Ottoman soldiers and spoke to him in Arabic speech which he did not comprehend. So he thought that he was aiming at him evil. Then he shot him. Then the Bedawi fled to his folk yelling ; and, lo, two of[6] the Bedawin who came on assaulting. So the soldiers shot them with the lead. Then they fell slain. Then the Arabs (of the desert) cried out one after another from every side, some of them summoning others to the revenge and to the seizing upon the vengeance, and

---

[1] the Excellency of.   [2] Power.   [3] pl.   [4] impf.   [5] narratives in its arriving unto.   [6] (we were) with two from.

there almost befell a very great[1] sedition, had not[2] the two sherifs entered into negociations with the sheikhs of the Arabs (of the desert) and not ceased dealing gently with them until they broke their enthusiasm and satisfied them with the paying[3] of the blood-wit of the slain, 160 guineas—and may God suffice the believers (against) the evil of the fighting.

49. Oneiza in Nejd.

Verily the number of the inhabitants of this town is near (from) three thousand souls, and their present commander (he) is Abd al-Jawad (Jeved) son of Salim.   And there is not round it sowings or palmgrove, and the whole of its traffic goes down to it from Al-Kuweit and India and the Hijaz.   And its people are at one with (in oneness along with) their commander and (in) an enthusiasm in regard to what is between them, which makes to appear upon them (the) courage; and they are endeavouring always after (behind) what will benefit and make their country to progress, and they are inclining much to him who praises them and praises their commander.   And there is not to the commander an income except what he takes upon the beasts of burden and upon some of the lands which are sown (in) the time of rain. And this town has been the cause of the contention which arose between some of the commanders, and there were through (for) it wars which continued a space not short (it is not short).

50. The Dearness in the Hijaz.

(In rhymed prose.)

In what preceded I mentioned not a little (a thing other than few) in the description of the dearth which alighted, and the dearness which dismounted, in the Hijazi dwellings; and what was of the drying up of the springs and wells, and the being

---

[1] elat.   [2] were it not for that.   [3] handing.

imprisoned of the rains, and the withering of the pastures ; and the alighting of the drought in every valley, and we acquaint you that the state of things is upon (in) an increasing, and the dearth in a becoming violent, whilst (and) the (nomadic) Arabs remove from their dwellings ; and take camel from their pasture-grounds into the cities and the villages, and especially into Mecca, the mother of the villages, in flight[1] with themselves and their children from death by hunger[1], and perishing (perdition) by starvation[1].

So we call to the people of (the) piety and well-doing and the masters of the gentle (sorrowing) hearts and haughty souls and the possessed of (the) bounty and munificence in the eastern parts of the earth and its western parts, that they stretch out the hands of help, and extend (stretch out) the palms of kindliness and benevolence (being conciliated), for the making light the woes of this dark calamity (alighting thing) between which and the reaping of the spirits of these pure souls by the reaping hook of hunger and dearness there was not except two half-bow lengths[2] or closer, and the sending of what their souls are bountiful with to the prefecture of Mecca the Glorious, and the seat of the lofty waliship to distribute upon the needy, and God will not let be lost the hire of the well doing.

[1] acc.　　　[2] a half-bow of two bows, Kor. 53, 9.

PART IV

ADVANCED PROSE

1. Autumn in Manchuria.

The land excepting in the southern part of the Kwantung peninsula, remains exactly as it was left when the harvest was carried, no ploughing whatever being done, as it is desirable to retain all possible moisture for the spring sowing. Only in the neighbourhood of Port Arthur is there any attempt to sow autumn wheat. Elsewhere nothing is sown until April. It is thus comparatively easy to travel in any direction on the plains, independently of the roads or cart tracks, so long as no rivers or gullies are encountered. Almost all the rivers, excepting the Liau, are now daily growing smaller, and the water as clear as crystal, so that fords are everywhere increasing in number.

The Times.

(*Literal Version.*)

And the people do not busy themselves in these days with any agricultural work in the meadows because they wish by that that they should preserve to the land the moisture which is good for the spring sowings ; only that the farmers round Port Arthur make a beginning in the scattering of the wheat of the autumn in contrast to the other districts, for they (m. pl.) do not make a beginning in the sowing except in the month of April. Then it results from this at that time that the travelling in all the directions is free from the difficulties where the earth is open and the waters of the rivers are low. And in these days the rivers—the waters in them are becoming less then less and they are pure, crystalline, and there are many fords.

2. NOVEMBER IN MANCHURIA.

With November a decided change may come. The weather may continue fine until the middle of the month, or it may break earlier, with odd days of rainy sleet or snow. The roads become slippery with stiff, half-frozen mud, but the river-crossings are not affected, except that the water is icy cold for those who ford them. Towards the end of November the ice forms into floating masses and causes much trouble on the larger rivers, where at the main crossings wooden, temporary trestle bridges are often erected. Early winter ice, which will not bear the traffic, sometimes stops all local communication, if there is no bridge, as the sharp ice cuts the animals' legs and often lames them. Towards the end of November the ground is frozen on the surface, through which, wherever there has been mud or soft wet soil, the wheels cut and are jammed. This causes serious delay but does not altogether stop traffic.

The Times.

(*Literal Version.*)

And in November the weather sometimes remains fine to the end of the middle of the month, and of the permissible is that there should make a beginning the alighting of the snow and the rains, with the cold, whilst the roads become slippery with mud frozen, until it resembles clay. Then the rivers do not increase, and only there is difficult the crossing in the travelling upon the feet or by means of the swimming. Towards the end of November large pieces of ice swim upon the surface of the large rivers from which there is mighty trouble to those journeying, so that on the main roads they originate light wooden bridges every year. And were it not for the bridge, it would make to cease the crossing, because the waters will be frozen in a degree that the snowy layer will not endure the travelling of the man and the animals, then it cuts their legs, then they become lame. And in the end of November the moist ground will be ice, and the roads which were covered with the muds will become hard, frozen. Only they will not carry the carts, so that it will be journeyed with difficulty.

3. DECEMBER IN MANCHURIA.

From December onwards it will become daily more and more difficult to do any trenching and by Christmas-time the ground from Haicheng northwards will be very solidly frozen to a depth of 3 ft. increasing to 5 ft. as one goes north. The *maximum* depth of hard frozen earth at Mukden is 4 ft. in January. During the Chino-Japanese war the Japanese found it impossible to intrench on the plains, but on the stony hillsides they were able, with much labour, to blast out certain positions. It is, therefore, not surprising to learn that they are preparing for all contingencies by hiring thousands of Chinese coolies to fortify the Liau-yang positions against an attack from the north. The Russian defences faced in the opposite direction.

The Times.

(*Literal Version.*)

And as to from the (making) beginning of December, then it is not possible that the man should dig in those days, because the ground—there enters into it the ice upon a depth of 90 centimetres from Haicheng with the directing oneself towards the north, and it is permitted that the thickness of the ice should attain to about a metre and a half; and it does not exceed (from) a metre and 20 centimetres round Mukden. And the Japanese were not, in the course of the war between them and the Chinese, making intrenchments in the plain, but of the compulsory was at that time the fortifying of some of the places upon the hills by means of the stones. And for that you see the Japs taking into service the Chinese coolies to strengthen the places of Liau-yang from the forward[1] direction, because the Russian forts were directing themselves in the opposite[2].

4. The Army of Manchuria.

Have you ever seen a series of pictorial diagrams which gives you in a graphic manner statistical information with regard to all the countries of the world? In a special chapter dedicated to the military forces you can often find a table in which each army is indicated by a soldier, dressed in his national uniform, his height varying according to the comparative strength of the army. Look at Russia! It figures like a giant, while Germany reaches just to its shoulders, and the other countries rapidly dwindle to an average sized man. Japan looks like a dwarf and it seems as if the soldier representing Russia would only have to tread on it to crush it to death. Why in the present war has this not happened? What causes have aided this new David in conquering Goliath? Why has Japan inflicted terrible defeats on her opponent? It is the object of these articles to explain the reason, to examine the anatomy of the giant, to show the composition of his bones, his nerves, and his muscles, to diagnose the diseases that disable this huge body, and to demonstrate why the giant cannot deal the crushing blow to the dwarf.

The Times.

(*Literal Version.*)

Have you seen in the yearly almanacks and statistics figures representing the countries of the world? In the chapter of the military strengths you find each power indicated by a soldier, who has put on the uniform by which he is particularized, and his length in proportion to the number of soldiers in the armies

[1] facing.   [2] in another (self) directing.

of the country to which he belongs. Have you not seen the
Russian army figured in the shape of a soldier, bulky and large
of body, so that the one representing the German army scarcely
arrives except to his shoulders. And you have seen the
Japanese army represented by a soldier, insignificant, small, who
scarcely arrives at the thigh of the Russian soldier. All of us
have seen that in the books and periodicals. Then what is the
reason which makes to this insignificant, feeble one the upper
hand, and has expanded for him the paths of triumph over that
mighty tyrant? Nay, how slays David Goliath in the plain of
the eastern, greatest war?

For the answer to these questions it is necessary for me[1] that
I should take in hand to cut up the bulky (dead) body of that
tyrant and analyse its branches and set forth its members, in
order that I may make clear its reality and the amount of what
belongs to it of the strength and health.

5. COAL IN MANCHURIA.

The fuel supply for both armies will be a serious problem.
The coal mines at Wa-fang-tien and Yen-tai are both in
Japanese hands. They are none of them as yet very productive,
and we have not heard to what extent the Russians destroyed
the workings. The Fu-chun mines are much more valuable, as
there is a large supply of good steam coal readily accessible, and
if the existing mines are destroyed it would be a simple matter
to start others, following the common Chinese methods. Should
the Russians lose these, the loss will be very serious, as there are
no other mines of any special value northwards, except some to
the east of Kirin, which are far from the railway. It seems,
therefore, that the Russians will need to import Siberian coal for
their engines on the Kharbin-Mukden line, which are constructed to burn coal, or else use the engines of the Siberian
line, which burn wood.

The Times.

[1] acc.

(Literal Version.)

And of the serious matters is the question of the materials of the burning because the mines of the coal in W. and Y. are in the hands of the Japs. And of the supposable is that the Russians destroyed the ways of exploiting and employing them before passing them by, and there is not in them until now much advantage.

And of the chief of the mines in importance for the Russians are the mines of F. in which there is much good coal, and if they destroyed them, the Japs could dig others with ease as the Chinese do. But if the Russians were forced to vacate these, it would be upon them a determining blow and a chief loss, seeing that there are not found with them after that the sufficient mines except in the east of K. distant (masc. sing.) with a remote distance from the railway. Then they would be forced at that time either to requisition the coal necessary for the locomotives which travel on the line between Mukden and Kharbin from Siberia, or to use the Siberian locomotives which are worked by means of the burning of wood.

6. THE TURK IN EGYPT.

The Turk was the conqueror of Egypt and within the memory of persons still living behaved as such. But there are now but few pure Turks left. In the absence of fresh importations from Turkey, a process of Egyptianisation set in. Absence from the headquarters of Ottoman thought and action, and intermarriage with Egyptians, produced their natural results. It is thought that no such thing as a pure Turk of the third generation is to be found within the length and breadth of the land. It is, indeed, a misnomer to speak of Turks in Egypt. By the time the English occupied the country in 1882, all the Turks had blossomed or, as some would say, degenerated into Turco-Egyptians. This is a point which the English politician had to bear carefully in mind, for as each year of the British occupation passed by, the Turco-Egyptian element in Egyptian society became more Egyptian and less Turkish in character and habits of thought.

Modern Egypt.

(*Literal Version.*)

The Turk was the conqueror of Egypt, playing the rôle of the victor to the period of folk who do not cease until now—in the bond of life. As for now, then there have not remained of the Turks except some individuals, and when there did not come other than they of the original Turks, their Egyptianizing began. Verily their being remote from the capital of Othmâni thought and action and their mixing with the Egyptians by marriage led to the expected natural results. And it is said that there is not found in the length and breadth of Egypt a pure Turk. And he is mistaken who speaks about the Turks in Egypt, because they are other than found in it in fact. For when the English occupied Egypt in the year 1882, the whole of the Turks had progressed and become Egyptianized, or as folk say, that they had degenerated ; and it is an affair which it is necessary upon the English politician that he should remember it.

7. THE EGYPTIAN TURK AND THE SULTAN.

In common with other Moslems, the Turco-Egyptian looked to the Sultan as their Pope. But on the other hand they were year by year less inclined to regard him as their king. When, in 1892, the British government stepped in and prevented a Firman of the Sultan from being promulgated, they rallied in a half-hearted and platonic manner round the Commander of the Faithful. They winced at the spectacle of his humiliation at the hands of a Christian Power. But even then the feelings of

w.   6 indignation excited in their heart were probably no stronger than those which would be felt by an Italian patriot who was also a devout Catholic and who saw the Vatican obliged to yield to the Quirinal.

Again, in 1906, when the relations of England and Turkey were strained by what is known by the 'Sinai Peninsula' incident, a strong wave of pro-Turkish feeling seemed to sweep over Egypt, but it was a purely fictitious movement, manufactured by the Anglophobe press. It speedily died a natural death.

Modern Egypt.

(*Literal Version.*)

And the Egyptian Turks have agreed with the rest of the Moslems in regarding the Sultan as their religious chief, as the Christians regard the Pope. But they made less, year after other, of their inclination to regarding him as Sultan to them. Then when the English Government stepped in in the year 1892 and prevented the promulgating of the Sultanic Firman, the Egyptian Turks rallied to the side of the Commander of the Believers with a rallying feeble of resolution and displayed the spite of a (person) hurt, since they saw a Christian power humbling him. And with (all) that, then verily what was excited in their breasts of the anger perhaps did not exceed over what an Italian true of patriotism displays (and he is a pious Catholic also) when he sees the Vatican compelled upon the humiliation to the administration of the Government of Italy.

Next when the relations between England and Turkey became strained in the year 1906 by reason of an event the like of the Peninsula of Sinai, there appeared there a sentiment of strong rallying towards Turkey : then it was as if it comprised Egypt in its entirety : except that it was a fictitious movement, which the press hostile to England had manufactured, and it did not delay that it died a natural manner of death.

8. CHARACTER OF THE TURCO-EGYPTIAN.

The peculiar characteristic of the typical Turco-Egyptian is his catholic capacity for impotent hatred. He hates the Englishman because the Englishman curbs him. He hates and fears the pure Turk, because the pure Turk is difficult to curb. He despises the Egyptian whom he regards as his prey, and who, in fact, would be his prey were it not for the English watchdog who keeps him off.

Among the many vague ideals incapable of realisation which are floating about in the Egyptian political atmosphere nothing is more certain than that the ideal of the Turco-Egyptian can never be realised. He can never be restored to the position of trust, which he formerly occupied and abused.

Modern Egypt.

(*Literal Version.*)

And the most important of that by which this (person) is distinguished is his surpassing ability upon weak hatred. So he dislikes the Englishman because he withholds him from his passion. And he dislikes the pure Turk and fears him also, because as for the pure Turk—not easy is his withholding and the pulling up of his headstrongness. And he despises the Egyptian and looks upon him as a plunder for him. And the Egyptian would be like that if it were not for the Englishman who repulses from him, since he stands upon watching him.

Verily the hopes of the Egyptian Turk are the first of the hopes the verification of which is absolutely impossible from among the many imaginary hopes spreading in the sky of political Egypt. For it would be absurd to replace him in the position of charge which was formerly his, then he made evil the conduct in it.

9.   HIS CONVICTIONS AND HIS INTERESTS.

In truth religious conviction, backed by racial prejudice, and by the sympathy generally entertained amongst Orientals for a theocratic form of Government, may for a while wrestle with personal interest and political associations, but the chances are that, if the struggle is continued, religious conviction will get a fall.   Pro-Turkish sentiment will therefore smoulder and occasionally flicker up sufficiently to show some feeble light, but it will never burst into a blaze.   For, in fact, many considerations are constantly dragging the Turco-Egyptian in a direction away from Constantinople.   Although he may try to deceive others, he cannot deceive himself.

Modern Egypt.

(*Literal Version.*)

And the reality of the affair is that the religious conviction backed by racial prejudices and the general inclination of the Orientals to the form of the theocratic government perhaps have rubbed themselves against personal interests and political associations, but when this battling is long between the two principles, then the more preponderating (thing is) that the religious aspect will be hit with failure.   And necessarily so, for the feeling of sympathy towards Turkey—there will sometimes be to it smoke, and occasionally it will send up some flame sufficing to show a little light, but it will never pass over into a blaze, for there are many considerations which remove the Egyptian Turk from Constantinople.   And he, if he put himself in possession of the deception of other than he, then he does not deceive himself.

10.   THE TURKISH RÉGIME IN EGYPT.

He knows well enough what he would do if he got the upper hand ; he would plunder everyone he could indiscriminately. He knows that his own brethren, whom his ancestors left behind at Constantinople, are prepared to act on precisely similar

principles, and he feels that if they, who are certainly the most
powerful of the sons of Islam, were once to step on the scene,
his affinity of race would avail him little ; he would take rank with
the plundered rather than with the plunderers, or, at best, he would
have to stand by and see the Egyptians robbed without obtaining
any adequate share of the plunder.   Rather than submit to this
fate, it were better perhaps to take the good things the Englishmen
offer him ; it is true that they will not let him spoil the Egyptians,
but they will prevent the Constantinopolitan Turk from spoiling
him ; they give him wealth and security for his life and property ;
perhaps it will be as well to pause before throwing away these
benefits in order to obtain the doubtful advantages of being
governed by a number of co-religionists, whose community of
religion would in no degree temper their rapacity.

Modern Egypt.

(*Literal Version.*)

And he knows for certain what he would do if the vetoing
and the commanding extended[1] to him—that he would in that case
plunder every man and not refrain from one, and he knows that
his own brethren, who do not cease from the period of his ancestors
(being) in Constantinople, would not put off from setting about
the like of that, and he feels also that the Turks, and they are
the strongest of the followers of Islam without doubt, if they
took the affair in hand, the unity of his race-origin with them
would not benefit him at all.   Then he would prefer that he
should be among the plundering than among the plundered.   Or
he would be forced to stand still on a side and see the Egyptians
being plundered and their rights spoiled, without that there is to
him a share of those spoiled spoils.   Then he prefers that he should
enjoy himself in the good things which the English offer to him ; and
they—together with (the fact) that they prevent him from spoiling
the Egyptians—then verily they also protect him himself from the

[1] came to an end.

Turks of Constantinople. They enlarge to him the wealth and guard his life and properties. Then it is fitter in him that he should think twice before that he leaves (alone) all of these benefits by way[1] of the resulting upon privileges other than assured; since there will take in hand his affairs a section from his brethren in the Faith, whose religious community with him[2] would not make less of their quarrelsomeness and their love of gain.

11. THE BRITISH OCCUPATION.

Thus, in 1882, the English found a body of Turco-Egyptians who occupied the principal places under Government; who were the chief landowners in the country; who disliked the English inasmuch as they knew by intuition that their intervention would save the Egyptians from being plundered; who occasionally cast a glance towards Constantinople, and were willing enough to try and scare the English with the bugbear of the Khalif's spiritual authority; who would have been bitterly disappointed if their flirtations with the Porte had been taken seriously, and if the Mohammadan Pope, doffing his mitre, had assumed the crown, handled the sword, and commenced to assert his authority in temporal affairs; and who, lastly, in the presence of the alien and the Christian showed a tendency to amalgamate with the other dwellers on Egyptian soil in the creation of a sort of spurious patriotism. I say spurious patriotism, because the alliance between the semi-Egyptianized Turk and the pure Egyptian is unnatural. The people of Egypt are not really with the representative Turco-Egyptians.

Modern Egypt.

(*Literal Version.*)

And accordingly the English found in the year 1882 a body of the Egyptianized Turks occupying the highest offices in the Government and they were the largest landowners in the country

[1] in the path.   [2] and him.

and they were disliking the English, knowing[1] that the intervention of these English would rescue the Egyptians from the being plundered and spoiled. And they occasionally were turning to Constantinople and were using deceit to scare the Englishman with the phantom of the religious authority of the Khalif.

As for these, their hopes would have failed much, if that the High Door had solemnised their political efforts, then the Islamic Pope had put on his crown and bared his rapier, and begun turning (the mill of) his authority in worldly affairs. Thereafter verily they lastly in reference to the existence of the alien and the Christian inclined to mingle with the rest of the inhabitants in Egypt, and participate with them in a sort of the sorts of spurious patriotism ; because the alliance between the like of the Egyptianized Turk and between the pure Egyptian is not natural. And the truth of the affair is that the peoples of Egypt are not rallying to the opinion of the Egyptian Turk.

12. EGYPTIAN PATRIOTISM.

Then again, as time went on, a few Turco-Egyptians were animated by sentiments which, however impracticable, were by no means ignoble. They became identified with Egyptian aspirations and wished to establish a government free from interference of either Turk or European. A few also recognized the benefits conferred on the country by the British occupation and loyally co-operated with the British officials in furthering the cause of reform.

Modern Egypt.

(*Literal Version.*)

And along with the process of time a few Egyptian Turks became animated by sentiments which were not at all ignoble, even if to achieve them were other than possible. These Egyptianized Turks became identified with the Egyptians themselves,

[1] out of a knowing from them.

and inclined to their aspirations, and wished that they should
proclaim an independent government in the affairs of which no
Turk or European should interfere. And of them (some) folk
valued the goods which the English occupation had conferred
upon[1] Egypt with the due of their value, then worked with
loyalty along with the English officials to back up the reform.

13. THE GRANTING OF THE CONSTITUTION.

The dramatic rapidity with which the Sultan has granted a
Constitution to Turkey is the best proof of the imminent peril in
which he has found himself. For the moment it does not matter
very much whether, as is most probable, he has revived the
suspended Constitution of 1876, or whether as is apparently
suggested, in the official announcement, he has promulgated an
entirely new Constitution. The one momentous fact, which is
inevitably destined to have far reaching consequences in Eastern
Europe, is that Abdul Hamid has professedly relinquished some,
at any rate, of those despotic and autocratic privileges which he
abandoned almost immediately after his accession only to seize
them again with a firmer grasp. We have still to see whether his
sudden decision to liberalize the institutions of Turkey will suffice
to rescue him from the very grave plight in which he is placed.

The Times.

(*Literal Version.*)

Verily the sudden way which the Sultan has used in granting
the fundamental canon to Turkey is the most excellent proof of
the mighty danger in which he has found himself. As to now, it
is not much important if he has revived that Constitution which
he had suspended in the year 1877 (as it is the preponderating),
or had originated a code new from its first to its end (as is understood from the official advertisement). But the affair which is

---

[1] to.

worthy of the surpassing solicitude, and there is no escape that there should be to it a distant impression upon Eastern Europe—it is that Abdul Hamid has relinquished in some sort some of those despotic, responsible privileges which he had already left alone upon the trace of [immediately after] his accession: thereafter he did not tarry that he sought to return to them, and laid hold of them with a violent laying hold. It remains that we see from the vicissitudes of the coming events, if his sudden resolution upon universalizing the freedom in Turkey will suffice to rescue him from the abyss into which he has fallen.

14. The Turkish Revolution.

The avowed primary object of the Young Turkey movement, which has accomplished this swift and almost bloodless revolution, was to secure his abdication. Abdul Hamid has acted shrewdly in seeking to make terms with his people while there is yet time. With the army at his back he was able to trifle with the liberties of his subjects, to oppress the various helpless adherents of other creeds residing within his Empire, and to direct an administration steeped in corruption and notorious for inefficiency. When the army began to forswear its allegiance, he was at once paralyzed and helpless. The military revolt in Macedonia is only one phase of a discontent which has become almost universal in Turkey. Had the Sultan been able to send other troops to crush the mutinous soldiery at Ochrida and Resna and other places, we should no doubt never have witnessed this hasty promulgation of constitutional privileges. But the Sultan was driven into a corner.

The Times.

(*Literal Version.*)

Then already the chief goal which the party of the youthful Turkey has set before itself—and it is the party which has achieved this swift revolution which was not sullied with blood (pl.) was

that they should instigate him upon the abdicating. Only that
Abdul Hamid has taken the line of wisdom and cunning, so
hastened to make peace with his community before the passing by
of the opportunities. For he, when the army was backing him,
was able to trifle with the rights and freedom of his community,
and wrong those whom he found in his kingdom of the followers
of the rest of the other religions, and to take in hand the halter
of his government which corruption rendered hideous and it was
distinguished by its feeblemindedness and the fewness of its
efficiency. But when the army began to manifest disaffection he
saw himself immediately weak, he is not strong upon a thing.
For the military revolution in Macedonia is only one phase of the
discontent which has become general in Turkey. And had the
Sultan been able to send another army to pull up the armies
rebelling, we should indeed not have sighted absolutely what we
have heard now of the originating of the Constitution and the
granting of the rights, but they [the army] narrowed upon the
Sultan the paths.

15. The Cause of the Revolution.

A notable characteristic of the movement has been the
friendly attitude of the leaders towards the Christians in the
insurrection. The manner in which they have been appealing to
all creeds and races to work together is in entire accord with the
spirit of the new Constitution, which is understood to confer
equal rights upon all subjects of the Sultan. If the Young
Turkey movement, which has already obtained its principal
object, continues to be conducted on enlightened and pacific lines,
it may go far towards bringing about the regeneration of Turkey.
We cannot forget, however, that the real instrument which has
wrought this change is the Turkish army, and the predominant
influence in the army was discontent at arrears of pay and
conditions of service. Military grievances probably weighed a

great deal more with the soldiery than any desire for a Parliament. When these grievances are rectified, the support of the army may possibly become a somewhat uncertain quantity.

The Times.

(*Literal Version.*)

And of that by which this rising is distinguished is the clear inclination of the leaders with a friendly inclining towards the Christians. For their summons is to the whole of the races and creeds to the agreement in the work, conforming completely to the spirit of the new Constitution, which equalises between the whole of the subjects of the Sultan in their rights. Then if the free, who have acquired now their first object, persevere upon turning their movement upon this peaceful, wise manner, then verily there is no escape that it should contribute towards the resuscitating of Turkey. At the same time we do not forget that the unique mean, which caused this overturn to exist, is the Ottoman army. And that the chief impression upon the army originated from its discontent from the being in arrears of its pay, and the evil of its conditions. And the preponderating is that the evil conditions in the military service were more in impression upon the armies than their desire for the resulting upon the parliament. So when these cease, perhaps the dependence upon the army will be making lawful the doubt.

16.   The Moroccan Police.

The insecurity of the environs of Tangier necessitated the organization of a police force. It was necessary that this force should be a native one, and to all intents and purposes under the absolute control of the Moorish Government, lest the fanaticism of the surrounding tribes should be aroused and a fresh series of outrages take place. After some show of opposition the Sultan has placed the responsibility of organizing this police force in the hands of an experienced French officer and an Algerian subordinate. Captain Fournier, who has already had experience of Morocco and is a good Arabic scholar, has been at work for a month or more in drilling a portion of the Tangier garrison, and has succeeded in instilling some sort of discipline into the ranks. In order to give every appearance of Moorish control, he has introduced Arabic words of command in the place of the English ones formerly in use, and which were, of course, perfectly incomprehensible to the greater part of the soldiery and had become mangled almost beyond recognition in the course of years.

The Times.

(*Literal Version.*)

The disorder and want of security have ruled in the environs of Tangier so that there became of the necessary the formation of a force of the Police, but there does not go away from the mind the necessity of making this force unadulterated native and under the absolute control of the Moroccan government ; and, if not, the leaders of the neighbouring tribes would blow towards the insurrection and yearn towards the religious fanaticism, and a befalling of dangerous happenings would be a decree which there would be no turning back. And the Sultan showed opposition at the first beginning in the formation of this force. Thereafter he repented towards the correct and stipulated to one of the French officers the care in this affair. And this officer is an owner of experience in the conditions of the Moroccan country, and of perfect facility in the Arabic language. This (is) not to mention that he has spent about a (the) month in the training of the garrison of Tangier upon the observing of order, and (then) has succeeded in that with all the success. And this man has done well and generously in that he has not made the military expressions of the command in the English language, as was the affair formerly, but has made them in the Arabic language. And in this is what removes far from the clouds of doubt in the minds of the Moroccans.

17. THE VISIT OF THE KING TO THE EMPEROR OF RUSSIA.

The King has arranged to pay a state visit[1] at Whitsuntide to the Emperor of Russia at Reval, where he expects to arrive in[2] His Majesty's yacht Victoria and Albert, escorted[3] by two cruisers on June 9. This is the first official visit which His Majesty has been able to pay[4], since his accession to the throne, to the Emperor of Russia, with whom he is closely allied by[5] ties of friendship and near relationship.

The Times.

18. THE MOSLEMS IN EGYPT.

The Moslems consist first of Turks and Turco-Egyptians; secondly, of Egyptians; and thirdly, of Bedouins. A few Moslems resident in Egypt will thus remain unclassified: for instance, there are a few Algerians and Tunisians, who are French, and a few natives of India, who are British subjects. There are also a considerable number of Soudanese, an element which was found of importance when the reorganisation of the Egyptian army was taken in hand[6].

Modern Egypt.

19. THE QUALITY OF MERCY.

The quality of mercy is not strained,
It droppeth[7] as the gentle rain from heaven
Upon the place beneath: it is twice bless'd,
It blesseth him that gives, and him that takes:[8]

[1] purposes to visit.　　[2] upon the back of.　　[3] kept watch over.
[4] visit.　　[5] in spite of what is between them of.　　[6] And after that there will remain some of the Moslems, of them a small number from the Algerians and the Tunisians, and they are subjects of France, and some of the peoples of India, and they are subjects of England. And there is a large number of Soudanese, and there was to them importance at the organisation of the Egyptian army.
[7] falls one by one.　　[8] the pitying and the pitied equally.

'Tis mightiest in the mightiest; it becomes[1]
The thronèd monarch[2] better than his crown:
His sceptre shows the force[3] of temporal power,
The attribute[4] to awe and majesty,
Wherein doth sit the dread and fear of kings[5];
But mercy is above this sceptred[6] sway,
It is enthronèd[2] in the hearts of kings
It is an attribute[4] to God himself[7];
And earthly power doth then show likest God's
When mercy seasons justice[8].

The Merchant of Venice.

20. THE RUSSIAN SOLDIER.

The Russian soldier is still what he has been throughout history—a man without dash[9] or initiative or the fine frenzy of battle[10], but at the same time a man who will stand where he is told to stand till he is killed, and who is not panic-stricken by disaster or awed into submission by[11] the superior skill or courage or numbers of the enemy.   He does not know when he is beaten[12], and, if he does not expect victory[13], is equally unexpectant of defeat[14].   He plods on in a sort of dumb indifference to his fate[15].

The Spectator.

---

[1] adorns.   [2] the crowned king.   [3] is only the title.   [4] attributed.
[5] pride and greatness and the appropriation of kings arising upon threat and menacing.   [6] fleshly.   [7] praise to Him and exalted be He.   [8] and the crowned strength is only resembling and nearing God's when justice is adorned with mercy.   [9] venturesomeness.   [10] war-rage.   [11] nor does he submit out of fear from.   [12] conquered.   [13] the conquering.   [14] the being routed.   [15] He has the patience of the camel not complaining nor caring whether his fate be near or far.

21. PACIFIC PENETRATION.

With this idea in view, a loan of £2,000,000 has already
been advanced by the 'Banque de Paris,' the security of which is
supplied by the custom-houses of Morocco[1], where the agents of
the French bank are already employed in[2] collecting the interest
on the loan, no less than 60 per cent. of the receipts being set
aside[3] for this purpose. Although there was considerable
opposition on the part of the Moors to this scheme, it[4] has been
carried through without any disturbance, and, like most things
in Morocco, the opposition proved to be ephemeral[5]. There is no
doubt that this hold which the French obtained upon the finances
of Morocco will greatly assist them in furthering their policy[6].

...It is much to be hoped[7] that the forthcoming French
embassy to Fez[8], which is to leave Tangier toward the end of
this month, will have[9] some definite result, and that the able
French minister to Morocco, M. St. Réné-Taillandier, will succeed
in persuading[10] the Sultan that the only possible course to pursue
is to have[11] confidence in the friendship and goodwill of France
and allow her to assist in the restoration of his Majesty's influence
and in[12] the reformation of Morocco.

The Times.

[1] To realise this object the bank of Paris has lent the Moroccan government
50 million francs secured by the revenues of the Moroccan custom-houses.
[2] have already made a beginning in.   [3] and that is by particularizing 60
in the 100.   [4] And this undertaking, although it had met with violent
opposition.   [5] came to nothing with the passing away of time.   [6] And
of what there is no doubt in is that France's resulting upon the security
of her loan by the Moroccan custom-house revenues will assist her much
upon following out her policy in regard to it (Morocco).   [7] And of the
hoped is.   [8] the agency of France in Fez.   [9] arrive at.   [10] convincing.
[11] the straight course to follow up which is fitting in him is only.
[12] smoothing the way for her in order that she may restore the influence of
his Sherifian presence to the country and assist in.

22. CHARACTER OF THE EGYPTIAN TURK.

But with all this the Turco-Egyptian has some redeeming qualities. The glamour of a dominant race still hovers as an aureole, albeit a very dimmed aureole, round his head[1]. He is certainly not more corrupt than the Egyptian; he is more manly[2] and the greater[3] the quantity of Turkish blood running in his veins, the more will his manly qualities appear[4]. He is sometimes truthful and outspoken after his own fashion[5]. He has a rude standard of honour[6]. Go where you will in Egypt, if any bit of[7] administrative work requiring a certain amount of energy has been well done by[8] a native official, it will generally be found that the official in question is a Circassian or a Turco-Egyptian, who is probably more Turk than Egyptian[9]. The Turco-Egyptian can, in fact, still to a certain extent command, and that is why, with all his defects, and in spite of the fact that the class to which he belongs is generally Anglophobe— although there are some notable exceptions,—it will be found that the individual Englishman will get on well[10] with the individual Turk, and better[11] with the Turco-Egyptian than with the pure Egyptian, the Syrian or the Armenian. The northerner and the Oriental meet on the common ground that the English-man is masterful, and that the Turco-Egyptian, though less masterful than the pure Turk, is more so than the pure Egyptian. The Englishman belongs to an imperial race, and the Turco-Egyptian to a race which but yesterday was imperial. The English, Nubar Pasha once said to me, "are the Turks of the West." *Modern Egypt.*

[1] Then his head does not cease being copious with the hopes of a dominant nation, albeit they are very weak hopes. [2] he is more excellent than he in the attributes of manliness. [3] in proportion as exceeds. [4] exceeds in him the appearing of the attributes of manliness. [5] and bold in making to appear his opinion upon the manner which he knows. [6] to him is a strange opinion regarding honour. [7] however trifling. [8] and you see that it is complete upon what was desired by means of. [9] his Turkish nature will have conquered over his Egyptian nature. [10] find easy the working. [11] more of easiness.

23. The Mufti.

The Grand Mufti is the chief law-doctor of the country. He is a magnate of whose spiritual authority the temporal ruler of the country must take account[1]. Despotic Khedives and even, it is said, Suleiman the Magnificent have tried to force the hand or over-ride the decisions of the Grand Mufti, and like their Christian prototype[2], who tried to throw off the Spiritual yoke, they have generally been obliged to go to Canossa[3]. The English politician also has to recognize the Mufti's existence. When, indeed, the venerable old man, who at one time occupied the post of Grand Mufti, advocated as the most natural thing in the world[4], the crucifixion of criminals, it was scarcely necessary for the Englishman to raise his little finger in order to remind the Egyptian world that, although the onward tramp[5] of civilization might be heard but faintly within[6] the sacred precincts of the mosque, he was nevertheless standing outside its walls with his treaties, his newspapers, and, if need be[7], his soldiers, to assert the validity of anti-crucifixionist principles[8]. But although in an extreme case such as this the Englishman might impose a veto on[9] some barbarous act, he could not do much more[10]. He could not make the Egyptian horse drink of the waters of civilization, albeit the most limpid streams of social and judicial reforms were turned[11] into the trough before him if the

[1] Verily he is the Mufti of the Egyptian dwellings in legal matters. And there is no escape to the government from taking account of, etc. [2] those who were before them of the Christians. [3] failed of the like of that. [4] as if it were work unpremeditated, habitual. [5] sound of march. [6] in spite of the want of their hearing within...except a little. [7] if (when) the matter necessitated. [8] the principle of opposition of punishment by crucifixion. [9] get the mastery and prevent. [10] go beyond that. [11] made to flow.

Mufti condemned the act of drinking as impious[1]. Popes and other ecclesiastical dignitaries[2] have before now shown that they cannot be dragooned[3] into submission. Neither do Muftis fear red-coated soldiers. Moreover, they fear the wrath of the European press even less[4] than they fear redcoats.

Modern Egypt.

24. THE KADI.

I well remember the grand Kadi who was in office when I first went to Egypt[5]. His venerable face, long white beard, small hands, dignified mien, and graceful robes rendered him a striking figure. Such, I fancy, were the Pharisees who were members of the Jewish Sanhedrim. His manners were perfect, perhaps more so[6] than his judgments.

His successor was a younger man with a fine intelligent face. He arrived at Cairo with excellent intentions: he was going to purify his court of false witnesses, and he was delighted when he found that I was able to talk to him in Turkish, albeit very bad Turkish[7], on the subject. I welcomed an ally and awaited the result with interest. I had not long to wait. The Kadi soon came to the conclusion that the Egyptians were an uninteresting race. As they appeared to like the corrupt system to which they were accustomed[8] why should he kick against the pricks[9] in trying to reform it?

Modern Egypt.

[1] decided to pronounce the drinking unlawful.   [2] chiefs of the religions.
[3] compelled.   [4] as that they are less in fear of, etc.   [5] in Egypt at my first coming to it.   [6] more excellent.   [7] upon the littleness of my knowledge of it.   [8] There gladdened me the existence of my ally and I tarried waiting until when there had passed a short time I saw the Kadi he had been forced to confess that of which the cream is :—If the Egyptians have become familiar with a venal, corrupt system and were satisfied with it, then.   [9] goads.

25. SHEIKH ABDUL-KHALIK EL-SAADAT.

Sheikh Abdul-Khalik el-Saadat, a nephew of the last-named[1] Sheikh, is the head of one[2] of the oldest purely Egyptian families in Egypt. Napoleon made great efforts to ingratiate himself with[3] one of this Sheikh's ancestors, who was at first decorated with[4] the Legion of Honour, and on this treatment proving ineffectual to produce the required results, was bastinadoed[5].

The present Sheikh is a member of the Legislative Council. He is ignorant of public affairs[6], but by reason of the respect in which his family is held[7], exerts, or at all events, might exert a certain amount of influence[8]. I used to see a good deal of him at one time, but eventually, for reasons on which I need not dwell[9], I had[10] to drop his aquaintance.

Modern Egypt.

26. SHEIKH MOHAMMED ABDU.—I.

The late Sheikh Mohammed Abdu was an "Alim" of a different, and I should add[11], a very superior type to those of his brethren whom I have so far described. He was one of the leading spirits[12] of the Arabi movement. When I came to Egypt in 1883 he was under a cloud[13]. Good-natured Tewfik, acting under British pressure, pardoned him[14], and made him a judge. He did his work well and honestly[15]. Sheikh Mohammed Abdu was a man of broad and enlightened views. He admitted the abuses

[1] the preceding his mention.   [2] a family.   [3] to make to incline towards him.   [4] then he gratified upon him first with the badge of.   [5] until when he saw this treatment did not bring the expected result, then he returned and bastinadoed him.   [6] questions   [7] respected.   [8] then verily is to him, or it was being possible that there should be to him, a mighty influence.   [9] which there is no need to mention.   [10] saw good. [11] om.   [12] leaders.   [13] angered upon.   [14] the Khedive Tewfik pardoned him, through what he was moulded upon of the generosities of the characters and out of docility to the acting violently of the English upon him in that.   [15] and paid the fidelity its due.

which have sprung up under Oriental Governments. He
recognised the necessity of European assistance in the work
of reform. He did not belong to the same category as the
Europeanised Egyptian, whom he regarded as a bad copy of the
original[1]. He was anti-Khedival and anti-Pasha, not[2] that he
would have objected to a certain degree of Pashadom[3] if he could
have found[4] good Pashas, but in his experience he had met with
few Pashas who were good. In fact, Sheikh Mohammed Abdu was
a somewhat dreamy[5] and unpractical[6] but, nevertheless, genuine
Egyptian patriot; it were perhaps well for the cause of Egyptian
patriotism if there were more like him.[7] But, regarded from
the point of view of possible[8] politicians of the future, there
were some weak points in the armour[9] of Mohammed Abdu, and
of those who follow his teaching[10]. Mr Stanley Lane-Poole
remarks that an upper class Moslem must be "a[11] fanatic or
a concealed[12] infidel." This[13] dilemma, in a somewhat different
form, has presented difficulties to[14] those Christians who look to
the letter rather than to the spirit of Christ's teaching. It
presents far greater difficulties to strictly orthodox Moslems, who
look almost exclusively to[15] the letter rather than to the spirit
of their faith. I suspect that my friend Mohammed Abdu, although
he would have resented the appellation being applied[16] to him,
was in reality an Agnostic. His associates, although they
admitted his ability, were inclined to look askance at him as a
"filosouf." Now, in the eyes of the strictly orthodox, one who
studies philosophy or, in other words one who recognizes the
difference between the seventh and the twentieth centuries, is on
the high-road to perdition[17].

Modern Egypt.

[1] was saying that they made not good the imitation of European characters.
[2] and I mean by that not. [3] he would have shunned them and thwarted
them. [4] had stumbled upon. [5] moulded upon fancy. [6] seeing
opinions, not possible is the running upon them. [7] and (it were) of the
interest of Egyptian patriotism that the likes of him were many. [8] the
possibility of their being taken as. [9] But if we look at the armour. [10] teach
his doctrines. [11] one of two, a. [12] in his secret. [13] And the
like of this. [14] stiff climbs in the path of. [15] lavish entire care on.
[16] if it should be applied. [17] becoming to perdition without a doubt.

27. MOHAMMED ABDU.—II.

The[1] political importance of Mohammed Abdu's life[2] lies in the fact that he may be said to have been the founder of[3] a school of thought in Egypt very similar to that established in India by Syed Ahmed, the creator[4] of the Alighur college. The avowed object of those who belong to this school is to justify the ways of Islam to[5] man, that is to say[6], to Moslem man. They are too much tainted with a spirit of heterodoxy to carry far along with them the staunch conservative Moslem[7]. On the other hand they are often not sufficiently Europeanised to attract the sympathy of the Egyptian mimic of European ways[8]. They are inferior to the strictly orthodox[9] Moslem in respect to their Mohammedanism, and inferior to the ultra-Europeanised[10] Egyptian in respect to their[11] Europeanisation. Their task is, therefore, one of great difficulty. But they deserve all the encouragement and support which can be given to them[12]. They are the natural allies of the European reformer. Egyptian patriots—sua si bona norint—will find[13] in the advancement of the followers of Mohammed Abdu the best hope that they may gradually carry out their programme of creating a truly autonomous Egypt.

Modern Egypt.

28. MOHAMMED ABDU.—III.

In my annual reports I frequently spoke of[14] him in high terms, and no one regretted his premature death more sincerely than

---

[1] This and verily the.   [2] om.   [3] he founded.   [4] establisher. [5] in the eye of.   [6] or rather.   [7] But the violence of the doubting of the strict Moslem regarding them and his suspecting them of straying from the Faith prevent him from the travelling with them long.   [8] you see them generally other than Europeanised to a limit that they should attract to them the Egyptian imitating European ways.   [9] strict.   [10] going to extremes.   [11] his.   [12] with which it is possible to supply them.   [13] And every Egyptian loving his home will see.   [14] lauded.

myself. At the same time, I[1] must confess that I experienced a[2] shock in reading some of the revelations[3] in Mr Blunt's book. Mr Blunt's views on Egyptian affairs[4] appear to have been mainly based[5] on what he heard from Mohammed Abdu, whom he calls (*Secret History*, etc. p. 7) a "great philosopher and patriot." Notably I read with surprise and regret[6] the following statement of[7] Mohammed Abdu's: "Sheykh Jemal ed Din proposed to me, Mohammed Abdu, that Ismail should be assassinated some day as he passed in his carriage daily over the Kasr-el-Nil bridge, and I strongly approved[8], but it was only[9] talk between ourselves, and we lacked a person capable[10] of taking the lead in the affair." Without going into the ethics of Tyrannicide, it will be sufficient to say that the civilised world generally is disposed to look askance at patriots, and still more at philosophers, who are prepared[11] to further their political aims by resorting to assassination. *Modern Egypt.*

29. THE LATE SHEIKH MOHAMMED BEYRAM.—I.

I give yet one further sketch of a typical "Alim[12]." Sheikh Mohammed Beyram, who is now, alas! dead[13], was one of my best[14] friends in Egypt. He was, moreover, one of the most remarkable types[15] with which I have met[16] in the course of my Eastern experience[17]. He looked like a thorough gentleman[18]. I have rarely seen a more striking figure than that of this[19] grave Oriental, with his high intellectual forehead[20], refined

[1] with mighty laudation, and I am the mightiest of men in sincere grief over his death; although I in the time itself. [2] what befell me of. [3] new announcements. [4] questions. [5] built. [6] shock and grief. [7] what comes by the tongue of. [8] approved his opinion and agreed with him. [9] the affair was restricted upon. [10] were not directed (by God) to a person. [11] do not hesitate in the like of embarking in killing. [12] I will speak now of a man, who was an Alim in all the meaning of the word. [13] who died, grieved upon. [14] dearest. [15] men. [16] I have been directed (by God) unto the being known to them. [17] pl. [18] om. [19] a person who turned my glance and my mind to him more than this. [20] owner of the high forehead, pointing upon nobleness and sagacity.

features, melancholy eyes, dignified mien, exquisite[1] manners, and graceful[2] costume, who would sit with me by the hour[3] and sing a dirge over the decadence of Islam. Moreover, Sheikh Mohammed Beyram, not only looked a gentleman; he was one[4]. In no country have I come across a man of more elevated and refined feelings[5], or one whose opinions and actions were less tainted with worldly self-interest[6] than this Tunisian aristocrat.

Modern Egypt.

30. Sheikh Mohammed Beyram.—II.

Few things have given me a more unfavourable impression of native Egyptian society than that[7] the fine qualities of this really eminent man—whose appearance and character were alike remarkable, whose private life was irreproachable[8], whose religious faith was founded on a rock, whose patriotism was enlightened, and whose public aims were noble[9]—should have been scarcely recognized by[10] the herd of Pashas, place-hunters[11], and greedy Sheikhs, who were not worthy to unloose the latchet of his shoe. When he went down to his grave, none but a few knew that a star, which under happier auspices might perhaps have been of some magnitude[12], had fallen from the political firmament of Egypt, or

[1] high.   [2] beautiful, arranged.   [3] pl.   [4] was not generous of character (gentleman) in his appearance only, nay he was like that in truth.   [5] man excelling in the loftiness and polish of his feelings.   [6] less connected with selfish worldly interests than he.   [7] Verily the chief of the things which were awakening my gloom and impressed in me an evil impression of (from) the social Egyptian patriotic aspect—it is that.   [8] and he was the man remarkable in his outward and in his characters, the pure of page the clean of spirit in his private life.   [9] and he was enlightened of insight in the correctness of his patriotism, upon honour and skill in his public aims.   [10] a thing mentioned with.   [11] lovers of offices.   [12] and if there had been decreed to it circumstances more excellent (*masc. sing.*), it would indeed have been more in brilliance and magnitude.

perhaps, it would be more correct to say[1], of Islam. Pope's fine lines well describe[2] my honoured friend:

> Statesman, yet friend[3] to truth, of soul sincere,
> In action faithful, and in honour clear!
> Who broke no promise, served[4] no private[5] end,
> Who gained no title[6], and who lost no friend.

Modern Egypt.

31. SHEIKH MOHAMMED BEYRAM.—III.

Mohammed Beyram was a devout Moslem.   His faith was far more earnest than that of Mohammed Abdu, and men of similar type[7]. The subject which mainly interested him[8] was how to bring Islam and its ways into harmony with modern society ; in other words how to[9] square the circle; and in discussing the sundry and manifold branches of this subject with him, any tendency to disparage the Mohammedan religion at once disappeared[10]. From the point of view of the moralist, criticism cannot be directed against[11] the fundamental principles of the faith, but only against the abuses which have sprung up and which now obscure its primitive simplicity. Mohammed Beyram, regarded[12], not as a practical politician, but as a believer in the faith of Islam, was, in fact, a type of the best class of Moslem, a type which is, unfortunately, of rare occurrence. He looked sadly over a world which appeared to him to have gone mad[13]; he saw all that was noble in the faith which he revered stifled by parasitic growths[14]; he noted that Islam was tottering to its fall by reason of internal decay; he did not so much fear[15] the advance of needy disreputable[16] Europe, for he knew

---

[1] nay, I shall be truth speaking rather if I say   [2] are the best of that which there is described by it.   [3] loving. [4] sought. [5] selfish. [6] byname or rank.   [7] on his model.   [8] the chief subject he was interested in. [9] it (is) the planning a way to the reconciling between Islam and its customs and between contemporary society ; and, by another expression, he wished to.   [10] Then I was…forgetting any inclination to disparage.   [11] there is no path to the criticism of.   [12] and if we look at Mohammed Beyram. [13] he saw it, the *jinn* had subdued over it.   [14] the intruder who grew up and flourished around it. [15] His chief fear was not from. [16] mistress of ill-fame.

that, though the Moslem might be robbed and cheated, there was still a hope for Islam so long as its moral code and the material benefits it conferred were only contrasted with the practice and principles of adventurers who were the dregs of European civilisation; but he knew that the tap of the northern drum, which[1] had been heard in the streets of Cairo and might ere long he heard in those of Stamboul, brought more than the dragoon and the rifleman in its wake[2]; his instinct taught him that the institutions, which his forefathers had cherished, must in time crumble to the dust[3] when they were brought face to face with [4] the lofty principles which were inscribed on the Englishman's banner. He was not blind to these things[5] and, albeit he still clung tenaciously to the skirts of the Prophet of Arabia, he cried out in the agony of his spirit[6]: "Where shall wisdom be found? and where is the place of understanding?" And the answer which he gave to himself was that delivered by the patriarch Job when the world was young[7]: "The fear of the Lord, that is wisdom; and to depart from evil, that is understanding." On that common ground[8], the Moslem of the Mohammed Beyram type[9] could meet the Christian, and discuss matters of common interest[10] without stirring the fires[11] of religious strife. But when the discussion took place, how melancholy[12] was the result! The Moslem and the Christian would agree as to the nature of the fungus[13] which was stifling all that was at one time healthy in the original growth[14]; they would appreciate in like fashion the history of its extension[15]; but, whilst the sympathetic Christian would point out with courteous but inexorable logic that any particular remedy proposed would be either inefficacious or would destroy not only the fungus but at the same time the parent tree[16], the Moslem,

[1] the echo of which.   [2] knights and soldiers.   [3] come to nothing.
[4] there face them.   [5] he saw there things with the eye of the keen-sighted critic.   [6] bitterness of soul.   [7] Job in the ancient time.
[8] So from this direction.   [9] manner.   [10] discuss with him about the common interests.   [11] (dust).   [12] saddening.   [13] redundant (things).
[14] growing with healthy growing.   [15] the taking root of that disease.
[16] advertising with crushing proof that every treatment prescribed is either

too honest not to be convinced, however much the conviction might cost him pain, could only utter a bitter wail over the doom of the creed[1] which he loved, and over that of the baneful system to which his creed has given birth. We may sympathise, and, for my own part, I do very heartily[2] sympathise, with the Mohammed Beyrams of Islam, but let no practical politician think that they have a plan capable of resuscitating a body, which is not, indeed, dead, and which may yet linger on for centuries, but which is nevertheless politically and morally moribund, and whose gradual decay cannot be arrested by any modern palliatives however skilfully they may be applied[3].

Modern Egypt.

32. The Sheikhs of the Sufis.

The Sheikh Abd al-Baki al-Bekri, the first incumbent of the office during my residence in Cairo was a small wizened man with a pock-marked countenance[4], who when I paid him my Ramazan visit, used to peer at me through a pair of cunning[5] little eyes, in which fear and hatred of his visitor seemed to be struggling for predominance[6]. I always felt that when I left his house, he cursed me, my race, and my religion, and I never entertained the least ill-will against him for doing so. When he died, his brother, a much younger man, succeeded him. It soon became apparent that a new Sheikh al-Bekri had arisen. When the spiritual head of a variety of[7] Moslem sects boasted of his acquaintance with Lord Salisbury and Mr Gladstone; when he quoted[8] Jean Jacques Rousseau to

other than sufficient for the curing or is inciting upon the killing of the redundant herbs and the tree together. [1] confessing to the argument, convinced by the proof out of reluctance from it, but he suffices himself with lamenting the doom of the Faith. [2] from all my heart. [3] and perhaps it will remain living unto other ages, but it is in the state of death from the (two) political and social respects, and there is no path to preventing its gradual coming to nothing by a thing of the modern sedatives and soporifics, however skilful the physician were. [4] on his face traces of smallpox. [5] the fill of them cunning. [6] om. seemed. [7] various. [8] the opinions of.

me on the Rights of Man in excellent French; when he indulged in platitudes[1] on the blessings of parliamentary government; and when he asked me to lend him a few books which might enable him to understand[2] the "philosophy of the French Revolution" then I asked myself whether I was in a dream[3]. Was this *fin de siècle* Sheikh, this curious compound[4] of Mecca[5] and the Paris Boulevards[6], the latest development of Islamism[7]? I should add that the combination produced no results of any importance[8]. The new Sheikh soon sank into political insignificance[9].

Modern Egypt.

33. MOHAMMED EL-SAADAT.

I can best describe another "Alim" by relating an anecdote about him. Sheikh Mohammed el-Saadat, as his name signifies[10], was a Seyyid, a descendant[11] of the Prophet. He was, moreover, wealthy and influential[12]. I happened to hear[13] at one time that he was raving[14] against the English. My experience had taught me that political opinions in Egypt are not unfrequently connected with[15] some personal grievance. I called on the Sheikh and asked him how he thought matters were going on[16]. Everything he said was very bad. I encouraged him to talk[17]. Then he burst out into a long tirade about the desperate state[18] of the country. Could he, I asked, point out any particular abuse[19], for it was difficult to deal with generalities[20]? Certainly he could do so; he had no water for a portion of his property, whereas he always

---

[1] brought weak opinions.   [2] that he might seek to become acquainted from them with.   [3] in waking or in sleep.   [4] uniting.   [5] Mecca from one direction.   [6] from another direction.   [7] last of what Islam has brought forth in its progress.   [8] between the civilisation of Islam and the West brought no result possessed of importance.   [9] there did not remain for him political importance.   [10] as is known from his name.   [11] of the offspring.   [12] effectual of word.   [13] it reached me.   [14] making evil the speech.   [15] frequently built upon.   [16] his opinion on the circumstances.   [17] clear up.   [18] began to overflow on the evil of the state.   [19] Would you please specify to me one (instance of) making evil?   [20] in generalisation there is obscurity.

108

got water[1] before the English came into the country. I inquired into the[2] matter. As I had expected, I found that the Sheikh's statement was quite correct. He belonged to the privileged class. Under the old[3] régime he always got water, although his neighbours often went without it[4]. Since the English engineers had taken the irrigation of the country in hand, they had recognized no privileges. All were treated alike[5]. The Sheikh had to wait his turn. Naturally enough, he did not like this levelling process[6]. Fortunately, shortly after my interview with him, the Sheikh's turn came. He, of course, attributed this to the exercise of my influence on his behalf[7]. I heard[8] afterwards that his language at once changed[9]. He spoke in terms of warm commendation of[10] the British administration.

Modern Egypt.

34. AUTUMN IN MANCHURIA.

The weather conditions in the Mukden district during the month of October approximate very closely to those which prevail[11] round London at the same season[12]. There is, however, but little fog during the nights, which are chilly, with heavy dews[13]. The days are bright and warm, and the air is generally fresh and bracing[14]. There may be a day's rain now and again, but usually October is fine and dry. The harvest will all have been gathered in, where not trampled down and destroyed, and the country people will be threshing on their open, rolled earth threshingfloors, treading out the corn with oxen, if any remain, or

[1] Then he acquainted me that some of his lands were forbidden from the water, and formerly he was irrigating them constantly.   [2] the reality of.
[3] preceding.   [4] were forbidden from it.   [5] they had denied those privileges to their owners and treated everybody with equality.   [6] resented from this work which equalised him with other than him.   [7] Then he reckoned that originating from my exertion in furthering his interest.
[8] It reached me.   [9] he changed his language.   [10] lavished praise on.
[11] resembling much its condition.   [12] month mentioned.   [13] the dew falls with copiousness and violence.   [14] As for the day, the sky in it is not cloudy, and the air is warm, invigorating, strengthening.

ponies, mules, and donkeys, who also drag round small stone or wooden rollers. The few small proprietors who own no animals beat out their corn with a rough flail. All winnowing and cleaning is done by throwing the grain up into the air. Northwards in the direction of Tieling, the conditions are practically the same as at Mukden, but the nights are colder[1]. Nearer Port Arthur the climate is equally dry, but milder[2], and there are often dense fogs in the early morning from the sea.

The Times.

35. OCTOBER IN MANCHURIA.

The thick coarse grass on the hills has not died down as grass does in England, but has hayed as it stands, retaining its nutritive qualities[3]. The finer grasses afford splendid pasture for the rough native ponies. The taller grass and scrub is in many cases burned, either purposely or by accident. A small spark and a gentle breeze will at this season often cause many miles to be cleared[4] in a short space of time. There are no woods on any of the hills within the sphere of the present operations[5], though there may be a small copse[6] here and there. This does not apply to the region in which the Imperial Tombs are situated.

The Times.

36. WINTER IN MANCHURIA.

Around Port Arthur the winter is less severe[7], the ground, at Christmas, being frozen only[8] to a depth of some 12 or 13 inches,

---

[1] Then if the man go up towards the north in the neighbourhood of Tieling, he finds the nights more violent of cold than what (they are) round Mukden.   [2] As for in the directions near Port Arthur, then the air in them is dry together with the mildness.   [3] As to the thick grasses which clothe the hills, then they will be drying, preserving carefully upon their life and nutritive qualities.   [4] with a soft wind suffices, because it kindles in them a terrible conflagration which gulps up a mighty expanse of kilometres.   [5] within the dwelling of the war.   [6] a few bushes. [7] lighter of tread than it (is) in the other directions.   [8] the ice only descends into it.

whilst the stony, loose soil can be more easily worked with a pickaxe. In southern Manchuria—that is, from Kai-yuen southwards—little or no[1] snow falls before Christmas, and should any come[2] it usually melts very quickly. The winter of 1894–95 was an exception, when the heavy firing was apparently responsible for immense falls of snow[3], and the Japanese constructed defences[4] with snow beaten with the spade and then cut into soft blocks[5] which were piled up into low bullet-proof[6] shelters. That winter, with its heavy snow and the consequently damper cold, was the worst within the memory of many natives[7]. If heavy firing really has any thing to do with it[8], it is quite possible that there may be much snow again this winter. Otherwise terrible dust storms will sweep over the country, which are often blinding and make it impossible to see further than a few yards[9].

The Times.

37. THE ADMIRAL.

Admiral J.[10] is about 50 years of age, rather[11] tall and slender, grey-haired, with mustaches and whiskers[12], a ruddy complexion, a pair of blue eyes and a high forehead. He is of German origin as his name and his features imply[13], but nobody is more Russian at heart than he, nobody is more bitter[14] against Russia's foes or critics, nobody is more willing to believe[15] that Russia is superior in every respect to all other countries. I remember that on my way to the Far East I once wanted to send a telegram to my

[1] scarcely.   [2] or.   [3] only that that has resulted in the two years 1894–5 and the snow fell continuously in great quantity, until the people were in mighty bewilderment and were saying, that this is originating from the vibration and trouble resulting from the strength of the explosions, and it is a thing permissible.   [4] forts.   [5] pieces.   [6] bullets do not pierce them.   [7] most severe many natives remember.   [8] Then if the snow is resulting from the cannonade.   [9] violent winds make the dust flow over the face of the country, which hinder the man from that he should see a thing before him.   [10] The admiral the first letter from whose name is *J*.   [11] om.   [12] beard.   [13] indicate.   [14] more of hatred.   [15] more of belief.

parents from a small Siberian station at which our train had stopped, but the post-master would not accept it on the ground that only telegrams written in Russian characters could be forwarded[1]. Of course I had to keep the telegram in my pocket, and as I was speaking of this to a fellow-passenger, Admiral J., who was near and overheard me, joined in and said with some impatience, "Do people in your country accept telegrams written in Russian characters? No, certainly: but we in Russia do accept those written in foreign languages; are we not more civilized than you?" There was much to answer to this, but how can you persuade a Russian that Russia is not, after all, the first country in the world[2]?

The Times.

38. Morocco and France.

The Sultan's authority scarcely exists outside[3] the walls of the towns. The southern tribes, although peaceful at present, are ready to resist any attempts of the Sultan to reassert his authority, and already the Government tax-collectors and such unwelcome officials[4] have been driven out of the country. In the north the mountain tribes, always ready to rob and pillage, still threaten the caravan roads, and even the environs of Tangier. The intentions of France[5] are pacific, and in order to pursue a pacific course[6] the utmost tact and discretion will be required, for it would take little to awaken[7] the fanaticism of the tribes

[1] but the official of the telegraph refused acceptance of a message other than written in the Russian language.   [2] Then when I sat for the talk with the officers I informed them of what fell from the postmaster, and J. was near us. Then when he heard my speech he drew near me and said, Do they send in your country telegrams in the Russian language? Then I said, No. He said, In that case do you not see that we are more than you in civilisation, for we accept the messages in the other languages in the larger stations. Then I did not wish to explain to him the difference between the languages nor make clear to him the position of Russia in the degree of civilisation.   [3] does not go beyond.   [4] officials of the Sherifian tax and other than they.   [5] the French government.   [6] take a pacific line.   [7] stir up (the dust of).

and set the whole country in a blaze[1]. However French diplomacy has adopted the one possible course—to attempt to strengthen the Sultan's position so that in the gradual restoration of law and order the influence of France will appear as little as possible[2].

The Times.

39. BRITAIN AND GERMANY.

Prince Bülow's speech was answered by a most able and trenchant[3] speech from Herr Bebel, the leader of the Social Democrats[4]. Prince Bülow's complaints regarding the state of British public opinion towards Germany were met by Herr Bebel with a reference to[5] the long series of those speeches of the Emperor which could not have failed[6] to excite attention and earnest surmise[7] in England. We venture to say that those who are endeavouring to bring about[8] a better understanding with Germany should not confine[9] their operations to working with Ambassadors and the members of the ruling class. They will, we are convinced, find a much more fruitful soil for friendship to spring up in among those who are represented by Herr Bebel.

Spectator.

40. EAST AND WEST.

One of the obstacles which lie in the path of the European when he wants to arrive at[10] the true opinion of the Oriental is that the European, especially if he be an official, is almost always in a hurry. If, he thinks, the Oriental has any thing to say to me, why does he not say it and go away? I am quite prepared to

[1] and you would not delay that you would find the insurrection had become general. [2] However the French government has made sure that this is the straightest course and most level road, then it has made its one concern the strengthening of the position of the Sultan, until in the gradual restoration of the codes and popular systems the influence of France in them should be veiled as much as possible by the personality and government of the Sultan. [3] cutting. [4] popular. [5] a regarding of. [6] no escape to them. [7] care. [8] come with. [9] restrict. [10] get information upon.

listen most attentively, but my time is valuable and I have a quantity of other business to do; I must, therefore, really ask him to come to the point[1] at once. This frame[2] of mind is quite fatal if one wishes to arrive at the truth. In order to attain this object the Oriental must be allowed to tell his story and put forward[3] his ideas in his own way; and his own way is generally a lengthy, circuitous[4], and very involved[5] way. But if any one has the patience to listen, he will sometimes be amply rewarded[6] for his pains.

Modern Egypt.

[1] arrive at the subject.   [2] condition.   [3] express.   [4] crooked.
[5] difficult.   [6] rewarded with a mighty reward.

GLOSSARY.

In addition to the usual abbreviations, c. d. a. = governing two accusatives: elat. = elative: om. = omit word in translating: pc. = *active* participle: *a, i, u* denote the vowel of the imperfect: 2, 3, 4, etc. indicate the derived stems.

Abased, to be ذلّ *i* to abase 4

Abasement ذلّة state of a. مَذَلّة

Al-Abbas العباس

Abbasid عباسى

Abd al-Aziz عبد العزيز

Abd al-Baki عبد الباقى

Abdul Hamid عبد الحميد

Abdicate نزل 6

Abdul Khalik عبد الخالق

Abd al-Malik عبد الملك

Abd al-Rahman عبد الرحمن

Abdu عبده

Abide مرّ 10

Abiding = remaining

Able ماهر

Able, to be طوع 10 to be a. to be done, pass.

Ablution وُضوء

Abode = shelter

Abolish = render vain

About (concerning) عَنْ, فِى

(nearly) نَحْو

About to, to be سَ

Above فَوْق

Abraham = 'Ibrāhīma (gen.)

Abrogate نَسَخ *a*

Absence بعد inf. 8

Absent, to be غيب *i* inf.

Absolute كمل pc. بشر pc. 3

Absolutely على الإخْلاق

Abstain عقّ 10

Abstinence زُهْد

Absurd مُحال

Absurd, to be حول 10 absurdity, pc. fem.

Abu'l Darda ابو الدرداء

Abundant غزير

Abu Nuwas ابو نواس

Abuse سوء inf. 4 مساءة : سَيِّئة pl. reg.

Abu Sufyan ابو سفيان

Abyss وَرْطة

Abyssinian حَبَشِيّ

Accept قَبِلَ a

Acceptance قَبول (Divine) رِضْوان

Access وسيلة

Accession = sit, inf.

Accident, by خَطَأً : acc. (opp. of substance) عرض pl. أَعْراض

Accompany, to صَحِبَ a

Accomplish كمل 10

Accord وفق inf. 6

Accordingly = for that

According to عَلَى

Account of, to take عدّ 8 : on a. of ل

Accountant حسب pc. 8

Accuracy دِقّة

Accustomed to, to become دمن 4

Achieve, to نجز u and 4

Achieving نَجْح

Acknowledge ذعن 4

Acquaint (inform), to فيد 4 seek to become acquainted with 10

Acquaintance = knowing with a personal knowledge

Acquainted with, to be عَرَفَ i, أَلِفَ a to be a. with each other 8

Acquire, to نيل a to a. for self نول 6

Acre عَكّا

Act, action عَمَل, فِعْل pl. أَعْمَال

Act deliberately ثبت 5 a. slowly أنى 5 a. unfaithfully, to غَلَّ u

Acuteness فَطانة

Ad عَادُ

Adam = 'Ādamu

(Add, I should) على أنّى أقول, or omit

Addicted, to be همك 7

Address, to خطب 3

Adequate share نصيب

Adil عادل

Adjacent to, to be ولى i

Adjoin (تلو) تلا u

Administration إدارة

Administrative إداريّ

Admirable حمد pc. pass.

Admiral أَميرال

Admit (not deny) سلم ب 2

Adorn, to حلى 4 جمل 2

Advance زَحْف

Advance, to زحف : (of time) قدم 6 : tr. 4 c. d. a.

Advancement قدم inf. 2 or 4, intr. 5

Advantage فائدة pl. فوائد

Adventurer أَقاق

Adversity نَكْبة pl. reg. to smite with a. نكب u

Advertise, to علن 4, advertisement, inf.

Advice مَشُورة

Advocate, to شور 4

Affair عَمَل ,أمْر pl. أمُور

Affinity زلف inf. 5

Affluence نِعْمة

Afraid, to be وَجِلَ a

After (time) بَعْد (place) وَراء

Afterwards ثمّ ,بعدُ

Again ثُمَّ

Against فى ,على

Age (period) عَصْر pl. عُصُور : عُمْر

Agency وِكالة

Agent فعل pc. عمل ,وكيل pc. to make a. وكل 2

Agha اغا pl. اغوات

Agitate قلق 4

Agitated, to be قلقل 2 هيج 5

Agnostic لاأُدرىّ

Ago (long ago) : قَبْلُ ,مُنْذُ منذ زمان

Agree (with) 6 وفق 8 وطأ 6 وفق 3 inf. وفاق agreement, inf. 8

Agriculture زراعة agricultural زراعى

Ahmad احمد

Aid ازر 3

Aim مقصد

Aim, to قصد i

Air هَواء

Aiyubi أيوبى

Al-Akhdar الاخضر

Al-Ala العُلى

Albeit رغما عن ,ولكن

Albert البرت

Alexander الإسْكَنْدَر

Algerian الجزائرى

Ali علىّ

Alien أجنبى

Aligari عليكره

Alight نزل i inf. نُزول

Alightingplace مَنْزِل

Alim عالِم

Alive حَىّ to keep a. 2

All كُلّ : (not) at all = a thing : all of جميع it is all one to سَواء على

Allah الله

Allegiance to, to swear بيع 3

Alliance, وحد inf. 8

Allow, to أَذِنَ a inf. إِذْن to ask to be allowed 10

Allusion رَمْز in a. to, acc.

Ally نصير, حَليف pl. حلفاء

Almanac قوم inf. 2

Almost كُود a

Alms صَدَقَة

Alms, to give صدق 5

Along with مَعَ

Already قَدْ

Also أَيْضًا

Alter (document), to حرّف 2

Although وَإِن, على أَن, مع أَن

Altogether كافَّةً

Always دائمًا

Ambassador سفير pl. سفراء

Amend (رعو) رعا 9

American اميركي

Among بَيْن

Amongst عِنْد

Amount قَدْر, مِقْدار a certain a. = a thing

Amount to = attain

Amr عمرو

Amram = 'Imrāna (gen.)

Anak عنق

Analyse حلّ 2

Ancestry, Ancestor سَلَف pl. أَسْلاف

Anchor, to (رسو) رسا 4

Ancient قَديم pl. قدماء anciently, acc. s.

Ancientness قِدْم

Anecdote حِكاية

Angel مَلْأَك

Anger غَضَب

Anglophobe = hostile to England

Angry, to be غَضِبَ a to be angered, impers. pass. to make a. 4

Animal حَيَوان (domestic) بهيمة

Animate لهم 4

Annihilate دمر 2

Announce نبأ 2

Announcement نَبَأ

Annoyed, to be ضَجِرَ a inf. ضَجَر

Annual سنوى

Another = other : one another بعض بعض

Answer جواب

Answer جوب 4 and 10 a. favourably 4

Ant ذَرّة

Antar عنترة

Anti- = enemy of

Anticipate سَبَقَ i

Antidote دِرْياق

Antiques أَنتيكة

Anusharwan = 'Anūsharwānu

Anxious شفق pc. 4

Anxiousness شَفَقَة

Any مِنْ, أَىّ or om.

Apartment بَهو

Apostle رَسُول pl. رُسُل

Apparel ثَوْب

Appear, become apparent ظهر a
لوح , ظُهُور a inf. ظهَر u to
make to a. ظهَر 4 بدو 4

Appearance منظر

Appellation نِسبة

Appetite, to have an شهو 8

Apply (epithet) to نسب إلى

Appoint قوم 4

Appreciate درك 4

Approach (دنو) دنا u with مِن
to make to a. 4

Appropriation بدّ inf. 10

Approve حسن 10, approval, inf.

April ابريل

Apron ثِغال

Arab (nomadic) أَعْرابِىّ coll.
أعراب

Arabi عرابى

Arabic عرابىّ

Arabs (of desert) عَرَب, عُرْبان

Arbitrator حكم pass. pc. 2

Arch عَقْد pl. عُقُود

Area رحبة pl. رِحاب

Arena مَيْدان

Argue with, to حجّ 3 to a. with
one another 6

Argument حُجّة

Arise قوم u

Aristocrat شريف

Aristotle ارسطاطاليس

Armenian أُرْمَنى

Armour نسيج

Arms سلاح

Army جَيْش, عَسْكَر pl. جيوش
جند pl. جنود

Around حَوال dual

Arouse حرك 2 هيج 2

Al-Arqam الأَرقم

Arrange رتب 2

Arrangement تقن inf. 4

Arrears, to be in, اخر 5

Arrest قبض with على (attention) وقف 10

Arrive وَصَلَ i inf. وُصُول

Arrow سهم pl. سِهام

Arsuf ارسوف

Art مَعْرِفة pl. معارف

Article مَقالة pl. reg.

Articulate نطق i

As كَمَا as for, as to أمَّا as if كَأَنّ it is (was) as if كَأنّما as yet = until now

Al-As العاص

Ascalon اسقلان

Ascend (علو) علا u (gradually) رَقَى a ascent, pass. pc. 8

Ascetic نسك pc., pl. نُسّاك

Ashamed, to be حى 10

Ask سَأَلَ a c. d. a.

Askance, to look at رمق شُزْرًا u نظر شزرا u

Aspect (side) وُجْهة هَيْئة

Aspiration قَصْد, غَرَض, مَطْلَب طَمَع

Ass حمار pl. خُمُر

Assail بَطَشَ i

Assassinate فَتْك inf. ب

Assault هجم

Assemblage ندو pc., pl. أُنْدِية

Assemble جَمَعَ a intr. 8

Assert زَعَمَ u ايد 2

Assign (a date) أجل 2

Assist عون 4 one another سعد 3 عون 6 : to ask for assistance 10 : Assistance, inf.

Associate خلط pc. 3 عشر pc. 3

Association مُقارَنة pl. reg.

Assure ضَمِنَ a

Astronomer فَلَكِىّ

At مِنْ, لِ, فِى, عِنْد

Attack (renewed) كَرّة

Attack, to حَمَلَ على i

Attain to بَلَغَ u inf. بُلُوغ to make to a. 4

Attainment مَبْلَغ

Attempt جرب inf. 2

Attend وعى i to a. to عنى ب 8

Attention نبه inf. 8

Attract جذب i

Attribute صفة pl. reg.

Attribute, to نسب i u

Auf عوف

August أغسطس

Auspicious يمن pc. pass.

Austria اوستريا

Authority سُلْطة, سَطْوة

Autonomous = always independent

Autumn خَريف

Avail غنى عن 4 جدو 4

Available نجع pc.

Average وسط pc. 5

Await نظر الى 8

Awake, tr. يقظ 4 intr. 5

Awaken بعث على

Azhar Mosque, the الجامع الازهر

Azm-Zadeh عظم زاده

Babylon = Bābilu

Back pl. ظَهُور ظَهْر

Back, to أيد 2

Bad ردىء

Al-Badai' البدائع

Badge وسام

Bagdad بَغْدَادُ

Balance وزن 3

Ball pl. أُكَر أُكْرة

Bamboo خَيْزُران

Bane آفة

Baneful أذى pc. 4

Bank (of river) بنك عُدْوة

Banner راية

Barbarous بربرى

Barber حَلَّاق

Bare, to جرد u

Barley شَعير

Barmak برمك

Barzakh = Barzakhun

Basin طَسْت

Basis قاعدة

Basmalah بسملة

Al-Basrah البصرة

Bastinado جَلْد

Bath حَمّام

Battling عراك

Be كون u gen. om.

Beans فُول

Bear (child) وَلَد i (carry) حمل 8

Beard لِحْية

Beast بهيمة beasts of burden بَعير

Beat دقّ i ضَرَب u

Beating ضَرْب beating-place مَضْرِب

Beat out (with flail) خبط i

Beautiful جميل

Beautify حسن 2

Beauty حُسْن

Because لأنَّ

Become صبح i صير 4

Bed pl. فُرُش فراش

Bedawi بَدَوىّ coll. بَدْو (Bedouins)

Befall وقع عرا (عرو) *a* *u* to think
a thing will befall وقع 5

Befit جدُر ب *u*

Before (time) قبل, مِن قبْل
(place) أمَام, قُدّام before his
eyes نصُب عينيه

Beggar سأل pc.

Begin جَعَل *a* *u* أخذ *a* بدأ *a*

Beginning مَبدأ to make a b.
بادِيَ بَدْء .8 at the first b. بدأ

Behave سلك *u*

Behaviour مَسْلَك

Behind خَلْف, وَراء

Behold ! إذا

Behove بغى 7

Bekri بكرى

Belie جَحَد *a*

Belief عقد inf. 8 : = faith

Believe أمِن 4 believer, pc.

Belly جَوْف, بَطْن pl. بُطون

Belong = be (to a school) نمى 8

Belongings مَتاع

Below دُون

Beneath تَحْت, من تحت

Beneficent فيد pc. 4

Benefit فائدة, مَنْفَعة, خير

Benefit, to نفع 4 فيد *a* pass. 8

Bequeath خلف 2

Bereaved (mother) تُكْلَى

Bereavement ثُكْل

Bereft فقد pc. pass.

Beseech دعا (دعو) *u*

Besides سِوى

Besiege حصر 3

Best حسن elat. فضل elat. خير
at best = at most

Bestir oneself نبه 8

Bestow خول 2 مِنّ *u*

Betake oneself سَعى *a*

Better خَيْر

Between بَيْن

Beware, see Ware

Bewildered, to be دَهِش *a* to
bewilder 2 bewilderment,
inf. 7

Bewitch سحر *a*

Bey بَك

Beyond, to go عدو 5

Beyram بيرم

Bias عاطفة

Billiard table طاولة البلياردو

Bind شدّ *u* (firmly) 2 قيد

Biography سيرة pl. سِيَر

Birds طَيْر little bird عُصْفُور

Birth ميلاد to give b. ولد 4

Bishop أُسْقُف

Bitter مُرّ b. herbs صَبْر

Bitterness مَرارة

Black سود elat. to become b. 9
to turn b. دهِم 11

Black, blackness سَواد

Blame لُوم, ذَمّ

Blame, to ذَمّ u لوم a blaming
لَوْمة

Blaze شُعْلة

Bless, to برك (فى) 2 حيّ 3 to
win a blessing, to become
blessed 5 to bless with (God)
رزق u

Blessing مَزِيّة مَزايا pl. ,بَرَكة

Blind (of window) سِتارة

Blind عمى elat. pl. عُمْيان :
عشى elat. fem. عشواء

Block, to سَدّ u

Blood دَم pl. دماء

Blood-wit دِية

Bloom رَيْعان

Blot out (محو) محا u

Blow ضَرْبة

Blow, to نَفَخ u inf. نَفْخ (wind)
هبّ u

Blue زرق elat.

Boast فَخْر

Boast, to فخر 3 b. oneself 8

Body جِسْم, جَسَد pl. أبْدان
(dead) جُثّة (of people) جُمْهُور

Bold جرىء to become bold 10

Bombay بومباى

Bond قَيْد pl. قُيود

Book كِتاب pl. كُتُب

Bored, to be مَلّ a

Boredom مَلَل

Bosnia البوسنة

Both = dual : كلا

Boulevards بولفارات

Bound (limit) حَدّ pl. حُدُود

Bound (in bonds) قيد pc. pass. 2

Bountiful, to be جود u

Bounty جُود

Bow قَوْس

Bow, to ركع a a bow رَكْعة

Bowl طاسة

Box صُنْدُوقة

Boy صَبِىّ

Brain دماغ

Branch فَرْع pl. فُرُوع

Brand, to وَسَم i

Bravo زِه

Brawl مُشاجَرة

Bread خُبْز

Breadth عُرْض

Break كَسْر

Break, to كسِر *i* intr. 7 (promise) خلف 4 (oath, covenant)
نقض *u* نكث *u* (wing) جنح
pass. break out فجر 7

Breaking (promise) خُلْف

Breast صَدْر pl. صدور

Bribery قَبُول رُشْوة

Brick لَبِدة

Bride عَرُوس

Bridge جِسْر pl. جُسور (the
Kasr-el-Nil) كُبْرى

Brigadier شور pc. 4

Bright باهِر

Brilliance لَمَعان, رَوْنَق

Bring = come with: أتى 4 c. d. a.
bring forth نتج 4 b. together
رهق 2 b. upon ألف 4

Brisk, to be روح 8

Bristle قشعر 4

British بريطانيّ Britain fem.

Broad وسع pc. 5

Brother شقيق, أخ pl. إخْوان

Bucket دَلْو to lower a b. 4

Build بَنى *i*

Building بِناء pl. أبْنِيَة

Bulk حَجْم (most) غالِب

Bulky ضَخْم

Bull ثَوْر

Bullet رَصاصة

Bundle جُرْزة

Burden حِمْل

Burden, to أوْد *u*

Burn حرق 4 to b. up 2

Burrow جُحْر

Burst into flame أجّ 5

Bury دفن *u* b. alive وأد *i*

Bushel مُكَيَّل

Business شُغْل, شَأْن pl. شُؤُون,
أشْغال

Busy oneself شغل 8

But إلّا, ولكن, لاكِن

Butt نطح *a*

Al-Buwair البُوير

Buy شرى 8 buyer, pc.

Buzurjumihr = Buzurjumihru

By ب (oath) و

Byname لَقَب

Bypath برزيق

Caesarea قيساريّة

Café قَهْوة pl. قهاوٍ

Cairo القاهِرة

Calamity مُصيبة pl. مصايب

Caliphate خلافة

Call دُعاء

Call, call upon, to دعا (دعو) u
pc. pl. دُعاة c. on (visit) زور u
c. to ندو 3

Camel جَمَل pl. جمال she-camel
ناقة pl. إبل herd of camels
رحل a to take c. نَعَم pl. أنْعام

Campaign بَيْكار

Candidate, to make one a رشّح 2
candidate, pc. pass. Candidature, inf.

Cannon مِدْفَع

Cannonade = voice of the can-
nons

Canon قانون

Capable, to be قدر i

Capacity وُسْع to have c. for
وَسِع a

Capital (city) عاصمة (money)
رأس مال

Caravan قافلة, سَيّارة

Cards = gambling

Care عَناية (anxiety) همّة, هَمّ,
همَم pl.

Care, to بلى 3 inf. مبالاة

Carpet فَرْش i inf. فرش

Carriage عَرَبَة pl. reg.

Carry حَمَل i inf. حَمْل c. off
8 c. away ودى 2 to be carried
through نفذ u to c. out 4

Cart = carriage

Case حادث in that c. إذَنْ with
subj. إذ ذاكَ

Casing غلاف

Cast لقى 4

Castle قَصْر

Category عداد

Catholic كاتوليكي

Cause سَبَب pl. أسباب

Cause, to وجب 4

Cave مَغارة pl. reg.

Cease (with neg.) زيل a بَرِحَ a
زيل 4 a make to c. فتئ

Cell زاوية

Cellar كيلار

Censure ذأم a

Centimetre سنتمتر

Century قَرْن pl. قُرون, عصر

Ceremony كلف inf. 2

Certain, to be يقن 4 and 10 a
certain (time) معيّن for certain يقينا

Certainly بدون رَيْب

Chair كُرْسِيّ pl. كراسيّ, كراسٍ

Chalice صُواع

Chamber حُجْرة

Chamberlain فَرّاش

Change خَلَف

Change (alter) غيِر 2 to change nature of أَفَك i

Chapter (of Koran) سُورة (of book) باب

Character أَخلاق pl. خُلْق

Charge وَصاية

Charge (order), to وصى 2 and 4 to take charge of ولى 5

Charity (alms) زكاة

Charming شائق

Chase زحزح

Chaste (language) بَليغ

Chastise أخذ 3

Cheat خدع a

Cheer ضجّ i inf. ضجيج

Cherish علق 5

Chick-peas حمّص

Chide زجر u to be chid away 7, to be chid 8 pass.

Chief رئيس pl. رُؤساء كبير adj. عظيم elat.

Child, children وَلَد pl. وِلْدان, أوْلاد

Chilly = cold

Chinaman, Chinese صيِنى coll. صين

Choke (a well) طمّ u

Choose خير 8 to let c. 2

Christ المَسيح

Christian مسيحى

Christians نَصارى

Christmas عيد الميلاد

Church كنيسة pl. كنائس

Circassian جركسى, شَرْكَسى

Circle دائرة

Circumambulate طوف u

Circumstance ظَرْف, حال pl. أحوال

Cistern بركة

City مَدينة pl. مدائن, مُدُن

Civil مُلْكى

Civilization مَدَنيّة

Civilized مدن pc. 5

Claim, to دعو 8

Clan رَهْط

Clap (hands) صفق 2

Class طَبَقة

Classify صنف 2

Clay طين

Clean طهر pc.

Clean, to be نضُف to clean, cleanse 2

Clear بِيّن, بين pc. 4 ظهر pc. to make clear, بين 2 to clear up صرح 2

Clearing up of بَيان عن

Cleave to لزم a

Clement حَليم pl. حُلَماء

Cleverness مَهارة

Cling علق 5

Close دَنيّ

Clothe (كسو) كسا u

Clothes كُسًى

Cloud غيوم pl. غيم

Cloudy غيم pc. 5

Clover بَرْسيم

Coal فَحْم

Coarse (grass) خَشِن

Coat = robe

Cock ديك

Code دُسْتور, قانون

Coffin تابوت

Cold بَرْد, بُرودة

Cold, adj. بارد

Collect حشر u, i (debt) 2 حصل

College كُلّيّة

Colonization عمر inf. 10

Colonize عَمَّر u

Colour لَوْن pl. ألْوان

Column دعامة pl. reg.

Combat, to لقى 3 inf. ملاقاة

Combination جَمْع

Come, come to أَتَى i, جيأ i inf. وقف come across one مَجيء على i come back بوء u cause to c. b. 2 come in, on (arrive) قبل 4 come one behind other ولى 6 come out خرج u come over رهق a come up صدر u come upon جيأ i

Comfort راحة

Comfort, to عزى 2 comforter, pc.

Comfortable, to be طمأن 4

Command أمر u inf. أَمْر

Commandant فريق

Commander أمير pl. أُمَراء

Commence بدأ a

Commit crime جرم 4

Committee of Union and Progress جمعية الاتحاد والترقى

Common عمّ pc. شرك pc. 8 in c. جماعةً c. prayer = prayer in c.

Commonalty عمّ pc. fem.

Commune, community شَعْب (religious) جَماعة

Commune, to نجا (نجو) u

Communion مُناجاة

128

Companion صاحِب pl. أصحاب
to take as c. 10 the Companions (of Mohammad) الصحابة
Company = commune
Compartment غُرْفة pl. غُرَف
Compassion شَفَقَة with على
Compassionate رَحْمَن (رحمان)
Compel كره 4
Compensation كَفّارة
Complain (of) u شكا (شكو)
Complaint شُكْوَى to make c. 8 شكو
Completed, to be تمّ i
Completely تَماما, بالتّمام
Complexion لَوْن
Composed of, to be الف 5 composition, inf. 2
Comprehend فَهِمَ a
Comprise شمل u
Compulsion جبر inf. 4, compulsory إجباريّ
Compulsive ضَرُوريّ
Comrade رفيق
Concealed, to be خَفِيَ a to conceal 4 (keep secret) كتم u inf. كِتْمان
Concern, his one نُصْب عينيه (idol of his eyes)

Concern, to عنى i
Concerning عن, فى
Conciliate عطف 10 to be conciliated 7
Condition حال pl. أحْوال
Conduct صرف inf. 5
Confer (give) جزل 4 (discuss) ذكر 3
Confess عرف 8 قرّ 4 to force to c. 2 (doctrine) قول ب u
Confidence ثقة
Confirm ثبت 4
Conflagration = Burning
Conform طبق 3
Confound بهت a
Confuse لَبَسَ i
Congratulation فَرَح pl. أفراح
Congregate حشر u
Congregation مَعْشَر
Congress أمر pc. pass. 8
Connect علق 2 be connected 5
Conquer غلب i inf. غَلَبَة
Conqueror فتح pc.
Consciousness خَلَد
Consecutive تبع pc. 6
Consequently = on account of that
Consider فكر 2

Considerable = large

Consideration مَلْحُوظة

Conspire نجو 6

Constantine قُسْطَنْطين

Constantinople الإسْتانة

Constantly = always

Constitute قوم 4

Constitution دُسْتُور

Construct = build

Construction = originating : عِمارة (founding)

Consult شور 3

Contain ضمن 5

Contemn زرى 8

Contemporary = modern

Content قَنوع

Content, to be قَنِع a to c. 4

Contention نزاع

Continuance بَقاء

Continue ظلّ a

Contract عَقْد

Contradict خلف 3

Contrary, on the بالعَكْس

Contrast عرض 3 : in contrast to بخلاف

Contribute أدى 2 and 4

Control مُراقَبة

w.

Convince قنع 4 : pass. 8 : conviction, inf. 8

Convoke عقد i

Convulse زلزل convulsion, inf.

Cook طَبّاخ

Cool, to be قرّ a

Coolie = labourer

Cooperate = work with

Copious وفر pc. حفل pc.

Copiousness غَزارة

Copy (imitate) قدو ب 8

Coreish = Quraishun

Corner رُكْن

Correct صحيح, صَواب

Correct, to be صحّ

Correctness صِحّة

Correspondence مُراسلة pl. reg.

Correspondent كتب pc. 3

Correspond to لأمر 3

Corrupt فسد pc., to c. 4 corruptible 10 pass. pc.

Corruption فَساد

Costume زِيّ

Couch سرير pl. أسِرّة

Counsel نَصيحة

Counsel, to نَصَح a

Counsellors نُصَحاء

9

Count حسب *i* to c. up 8

Counting حساب

Country بلاد pl., pl. بُلْدان c. district ريف pl. أَرْياف

Courage شجاعة

Course (of action) خُطّة

Course of, in the فى أَثْناء

Court حُكُومة

Courtyard قاعة

Covenant عَهْد to make a c. with 3

Cover غطاء

Cover, to غطى *a* غَشِيَ 2 : to c. over ورى 3

Covering غشاء

Covet طمع *a* inf. طَمَع

Cow بَقَرَة

Cower جثم

Cradle مَهْد

Craft, to use مكر *u* crafty, pc.

Creak, to make to صرف 2

Cream خلاصة

Create خَلَقَ *u* وجد 4

Creation خَلْق

Creator خلق pc. فطر pc.

Creatures وَرًى

Creed مِلّة pl. مِلَل

Creep (into) سوب 5

Crime جناية

Criminal جرم pc. 4

Cripple مُقْعَد

Critic نقد pc. Criticism, inf. 8, critical انتقادىّ

Crooked عوج elat.

Crop غَلّة pl. غلال

Cross صَليب

Cross, to be برم 5 cross, pc.

Cross, to عبر *u* inf. عبور

Crow غُراب

Crown, تاج

Crown, to توج 2

Crucify صَلَبَ *i* Crucifixion صَلْب

Cruiser طَرّاد

Crush (argument) دمغ to c. flat حطم 2

Cry out صيح *i* to c. o. one after another 6

Crystalline بَلّورىّ

Cucumber قثّاء

Cultivate عمَر *u*

Cultivation عُمْران

Culture فَلاح

Cunning دهاء

Cupola قُبّة

Cure شِفاء i inf. شَفى

Curse لَعْنة

Curse, to لعَن a to invoke curses mutually 8 بهل

Custom عادة pl. عوائد

Customhouse كَمرك, جُمْرُك adj. جمركى

Cut قطَع a inf. قَطْع be cut off 7: cut up (body) شرح 2

Daily يَوْمى, adv. acc.

Damage عَطَب

Damascus دِمَشْق, الشأم adj. شامى

Damp ماءىّ

Dancing رَقْص

Danger خَطَر

Dangerous خطير

Dare جسر على u

Dark دلهم pc. 4

Darkness ظَلام

Dart نبل pl. نبال

Dash oneself صدم 8

Daughter بِنْت little daughter بنيّة

David = Dāwūda (gen.)

Day يَوْم pl. أيّام one, some day اليوم to-day يوما

Dead مَيِّت d. person مَيْت

Deaf صمّ elat.

Deafen صمّ 4

Deal, a good = much

Dear حبيب, عزيز (of price) غلو pc.

Dearness غَلاء

Dearth قَحْط

Death مَوْت, وَفاة, مَنِيّة to put to death موت 4: manner of death ميتة

Debar صدّ u

Debate with حور 3

Debt دَيْن

Decadence سُقوط

Decay حلّ inf. 7 لشى inf. 6

Deceit, to use حول 3

Deceive خدع a act deceitfully with 3

December دسمبر

Deception خديعة

Decide قضى ب i, بتّ u

Decision حُكْم pl. أحْكام to ask for a d. فتو 10

Decline to منع من 8

Decoration نيشان

Decrease نُقْصان

Decree قَضاء

Decree, to تيح 4

Decrepitude هَرَب

Defect عَيْب pl. عُيوب to lay the d. of upon عيب i

Defective, to be or make نقص u

Defence دفاع

Defend عصم i reflex. 8

Definite نهائى

Defraud بَخَس a

Degenerate حطّ 7

Degree دَرَجة to lead on by degrees درج 10

Delay, to لَبِث a to d. much بطؤ 2: to make d. 4: to think delaying 10: grant a d. نسأ 4

Delight نَعيم

Delighted, he was = it gladdened him

Deliver نجو 2: (a letter) = make to attain

Deliverance نَجاء a means of d. مَنْجاة

Delta دلتا

Demand طلب 5

Denier = dīnārun

Dense كثيف

Deny نكر 4

Depart بعد 8

Dependence عمد inf. 8

Dependency عَمَل pl. أَعْمال

Dependent تبع pc., pl. reg.

Depose عزل i

Deposit with ودع 10

Deposition عَزْل

Depth عُمْق

Deputation, to go, come on وَفَد i

Deride هزأ ب 10

Descent حدر pass. pc. 7: place of d. مَهْبِط

Describe وَصَف i Description, inf. وَصْف

Desert قَفْر pl. قفار to become d. بيد i 4 قفر

Desert, adj. بَرّى

Deserving جَدير pl. reg. more d. of أَوْلَى ب

Design, to عمد 5

Desirable, to be حبّ 10 pass.

Desire رَغْبة object of d. رغبة to excite d. in منى 2: to feel d. for 5

Desire, to روم u to d. eagerly رغب فى a to make to d. eagerly 2

Desist عدل i

Desolate, to be وحش 4

Despair, to يئس *a* to be in d. بلس 4

Despatch حرّ inf. 2

Despise هون 4 : 10 with ب

Despotic, to be بدّ 10 despotic, pc. or استبدادى

Destine, to قدر *u, i*

Destroy = annihilate or = corrupt

Determine قضى *i*

Deviate زيغ *i*

Devoted to, to be عطو 6

Devout ورع

Dew ندًى

Dhat al Hajj ذات الحج

Dictate ملّ 4

Die موت *u* : (of a Muslim) وفى 5, pass. he died a natural death مات حَتْف أنْفه

Differ نقش 3

Difference فَرْق to make a d. فرق *u*

Different خلف pc. 8

Difficult صَعُب ,عسير to be d. صَعُب *u*

Difficulty صُعُوبة pl. reg. عُسْر

Dig حفر, فحت *i*

Dignified مَهِيب

Dilemma حَيْرة

Dine غدى 5

Direct, to (God) وفق 2 : وجه 2 to d. oneself 8

Direction ناحية, جِهة

Dirge مَرْثاة

Dirhem درهم

Disaffection نَفْرة

Disagree خلف 8

Disappointed, to be خيب *i*

Disapprove هجن 10

Disaster فاجعة

Disbelief كُفْر

Disbelieve كَفَر *u* pc. pl. كُفَّار

Disclosed, to be فشا (فشو) *u* to disclose 4

Discontent ذمر inf. 5

Discovery كشف inf. 8

Discretion حفظ inf. 5

Discuss with بحث 3 حدث 3 نقش 3

Discussion مناقشة

Disease داء

Dish قَصْعة

Disinterested حسب pc. 8 disinterestedness, inf.

Dislike كَرِه *a*

Dislodge زَحْزَح

Dismiss, intr. فضّ 7 tr. inf. صَرُف

Dismount حلّ u

Disobey عَصَى i

Disorder خلَل, خلّ inf. 8

Disparage خفّ 10

Dispense غنى 4 to be able to d. 10

Disperse, to بثّ 2 بثّ u to be dispersed 7

Display شعر ب 4

Displease سوء u to be displeased سَخطَ a

Disposed, to be: om.

Disposition خليقة

Dispute with جدل 3 disputing جَدَل

Disquiet زعج a

Dissect فصل 2

Dissipate بذر 2

Distance مَسافة, بُعْد pl. reg.

Distant بَعيد pl. reg. to be d. بَعُد u

Distinct وضح pc.

Distinguish, to ميز 2 to be distinguished 8

Distressed, to be بئس a inf. بؤُس distress oneself 8

Distribute وزع 2, pass. 5

District قُطْر pl. أقطار : جهة pl. reg.

Disturbance شوش inf. 2

Divan ديوان

Dive غوص u

Diver غطّاس pl. reg.

Divert لهو 4

Divest عطل 2

Divide قَسَمَ i division قِسْم pl. أقسام

Divine إلهيّ

Divulge = disclose

Do فَعَلَ a do well حسن 4 do generously جود 4 to be done with فرغ من u, a

Docility قود inf. 7

Doctrine علم inf. 2

Doff خلع i نزع a

Dog كَلْب pl. كلاب

Doings أفاعيل

Dollar ريال وريالات pl.

Dominant حكم pc.

Donkey حمار pl. حمير

Doom مصير

Door باب pl. أبْواب

Double أضْعاف pl.

Double, to ضعف 3 to be doubled 6

Doubt رَيْب, رِيبة without a doubt بِدُون ريب, لَا مَحالة

Doubt, to ريب *i* to cause d. 4

Doubting شبه inf. 8

Dowry مَهر pl. مُهُور

Drag جذب *i* جَرّ *u*

Draught = drink

Draw near (دنو) *u* دنا

Dread خَشِيَ *a*

Dream حُلْم pl. أَحْلام

Dregs ثُمالة

Drink شَراب

Drink, to شَرِبَ *a* inf. شُرْب to make d. سَقَى *i*

Drive سوق *u* d. off نَبَرَ *a* d. out 4 قصى

Drop acquaintance = be cut off from

Drops رَشاش

Drought جَدْب

Drown غرق 4

Drum طَبْل

Drunk سَكْرانُ

Drunkenness سُكْر

Dry نشف pc.

Drying up جَفاف

Duchess دُوقة

Due حَقّ

Dumb بكم elat.

During خلال, مُدّة

Dust غُبار

Duty وَظيفة

Dwell سكن *u*

Dwelling دَار fem., pl. دِيار

Dynasty دَوْلة

Each كُلّ

Eagle عُقاب

Ear أُذُن fem. pl. آذان, أُذْن

Earnest = strong

Earth أَرْض (soil) تُراب

Ease, Easiness سُهُولة

East شَرْق eastern part مَشْرِق

Easy يَسير to make e. 2 يسر to find e. سهل 10

Eat أَكَل *u* inf. أَكْل

Eatables مآكل pl.

Echo دَوِيّ, صَدًى

Eclipsed, to be (moon) خسف *i* to eclipse, inf. خَسْف

Edifice بُنْيان

Edrei دَرْعا

Educate أدب 2 educator pc.

Education أَدَب educational ادبى

Efendi افندى

Efface تلف 4

Effectual نفذ pc. فعّال

Efficiency كفاية

Effort مَسْعًى make great efforts سَعَى a

Egypt = Miṣru: the Egyptian district القطر المصرى the E. الديار المصرية dwellings

Egyptian مصرى E. nature, fem.

Egyptianize مصر 2 Egyptianized, pc. 5

Eight ثمان eighty, m. pl.

Either...or إمّا...وإمّا

Elect نخب 8 (politically) صفو

Electricity كَهْرَباء

Elegy, to compose رثا (رثو) u

Element عُنْصُر

Elephant فيل

Elevate رَفَعَ a elevated, pc. 8 elevation, inf. 8, pl. fem. reg.

Eleventh حادى عشر

Embark (on ship) رَكِبَ a (on crime) 8

Embellish سول 2

Embellishment زَخْرَفة

Emerge نَبَغ a, i, u

Emigrate هجر 3

Eminent نبغ pc.

Emperor of Russia القَيْصَر

Employ عمل 10

Empty of خلو من

Empty, to فرغ 2 to be e. خلا a صفر u (خلو)

Encamp عسكر

Enchant سَحَرَ a

Enclosure حَوْش

Encourage شجع 2 encouragement, inf.

End آخِرُ (extreme, purpose) غَرَض (of time) غاية (goal) نهى 8 to come to an end نهاية

Endeavour سَعَى a inf. سَعْى

Endowment وقف pl. أَوْقاف

Endure حمل 5 endurance, inf. 8

Enemy عَدُوّ

Energy نَشاط

Engaged in, to be دأب a

Engine قطر pc. fem.

Engineer هندس pc. engineering, inf. هندسة

England الانكلطرّة, انكلترا

English, Englishman انكليزى

Enjoin فَرَضَ i

Enjoy oneself متع 5 let e. 2

Enlarge وفر 2

Enlightened نور pc. 5, نَيّر

Ennoble شرف 2

Ennui مَلَل

Enquire = Inquire

Enraged, to be حَنِق *a*

Enter دَخَل *u* inf. دُخُول to make e. 4

Entertain (feel) ضَمِر 4 (guest) قِرى *i*

Enthusiasm حَمِيَّة

Entire كُلِّيّ

Entirely جَمِيعًا

Entirety أَسْر

Entrust وكل 2

Environ ضَاحِية

Envy, to حَسَدَ *u*

Epicure رفه pc. 5

Equal سوى pc.

Equality سَوِيَّة

Equalize سوى 3

Equally على السوية, على السَّواء

Equip عَدّ 4 c. d. a.

Equipment عُدَّة

Equity نصف inf. 4

Erased, to be طَمَسَ *i*

Erect قوم 4

Err ضَلّ *i* to cause to e. 4

Error ضَلال an e. ضَلالة

Escape, no لا بُدَّ

Escape, to نجا (نجو) *u* فلت 4

Especially لا سِيَّما

Essence ذات

Establish نشأ 4 establisher, pc.

Etc. الخ

Ethics علم الأحلاق

Euclid أَقْلِيدُس

Eulogize قرظ 2

Euphrates, the الفُرات

Europe اوروبا, اوربا

European فِرَنْجِى, اوربى

Europeanized فرنج pc. 2 Europeanization, inf. 2

Even حَتّى even if = and if : even so = along with that

Evening أَصِيل, مَساء pl. آصال

Event حادِثة

Eventually = in the end

Ever أَبَدًا

Everlastingness أَبَدِيَّة

Every كُلّ

Everybody الجميع

Everyone كلّ إنسان

Evidence شَهادة

Evil (wickedness) شَرّ, سُوْء pl. سُوء (badness) شُرُور

Evil (bad) سَيِّء

Evil, to be سوء *u* to do, make e. 4

Exactly, om.

Exaggerate بلغ 3

Exalt علو 4 exalted be He, pf. 6

Example, for مَثَلًا to take e. عبر 8

Exceed زيد عن, على *i*

Excel فضل *u* to make to e. 2 to vie in excellence 3

Excellence فَضْل

Excellency جَلالة

Excellent بليغ

Except إلّا

Exception ثنى inf. 10

Excess فرط inf. 4

Exchange, to بدل 2 to e. mutually 6 to give in e. 4 to take in e. 10

Excited, to be هيج *i* excited, pc. to excite 2

Excuse عذر *i* to e. oneself 8

Exert oneself جَدّ *u i*

Exertion سَعْى

Exhausted, to be نفد *a* inf. نَفاد to become e. inf. فُروغ

Exhibit عرض *i*

Exhibition مَعْرِض

Exhort وَعَظ *i* exhorter, pc. pl. وُعّاظ

Exhortation عِظة

Exile غُرْبة

Exist = be: cause to e. وجد 4

Existence وُجُود

Expand مهد 2 سبغ 4

Expanse مَسْطَح

Expect = wait: to be expecting ربص 5

Expenses نَفَقة pl. reg.

Experience اختبار, خِبْرة

Experiment تجربة pl. تجارب

Explain فسر 2

Explanation بَيان

Explode فجر 7

Exploit غلّ 10

Explosion صدم inf. 6

Export صدر 2

Express عبر عن 2

Expression (phrase) عبارة لَفْظ

Extensive فيح elat.

Extent, to a certain = a thing

Exterior عَلانية

Extinguish طفئ 4 pass. 7

Extort غصب 8

Extract خرج 10

Extreme = end

Extreme, adj. ندر pc.

Extremes, to go to 3 غلو

Extremity طَرف pl. أطراف

Extrude 4 زعج

Eye عَيْن pl. أعْيُن

Face وَجْه pl. وُجوه (of building) بإزاء f. to f. with وَجْهة to lie on one's f. 3 سلطح

Face, to 3 قبل

Facilitation سهل inf. 2

Facility لين inf. 4

Fact وقيعة in f. فِعْلًا the f. that, om.

Fail بور u (of hope) خيب i, خور u (of strength) عجز عن

Failure فَشُل

Faint: he fainted = it was covered upon him

Fair حَسَن

Fairly, to act 4 قسط

Faith إيمان, دين

Faithful أمن, أمين pc. 4

Fall وَقَع a inf. وُقوع (of snow) نزل i (of star) هبط i f. down خرّ i f. heavily (snow) هطل i f. one by one (rain, dew) سقط 5 f. into ruin هدم 6

False بطل pc. to declare f. كذب 2

Falsehood كَذِب

Fame سُمْعة

Famed شهير to be f. شهر 8

Familiar with, to be ألِف a

Family عائلة, عيال pl. reg. (of Mohammad, etc.) آل

Famous شهر pc. pass.

Fanatic عصب pc. 5 fanaticism, inf.

Fancy خَيال

Fancy, to خيل a I fancy إخال to f. a thing خيل 2

Far قصو pc.

Far, adv. = by much: so far قد

Far East = furthest East

Farewell, and farewell = and the peace

Farmer فَلّاح

Fashion طَرز in like f. = equally: after this f. من هذا القَبيل

Fashion, to صور 2

Fast صوم u

Fasten شدّ u

Fatal موت pc. 4 قتل pc.

Fate حَتْف the Fates المَنايا

Father أب pl. آباء

Fault ذُنُوب .pl ذَنْب

Favour نِعْمة to show f. نعِم 4

Fear خُوف, مَخافة

Fear, to خَوْف, رَهِبَ a inf. خَوْف a

Feast (banquet) وَليمة (sacred) عيد

Feathers ريش

Features ملامِح .pl

Feeble خور, ضَئيل pc.

Feeblemindedness سَخافة

Feed, tr. طعِم 4 : intr. (animals) علف 8

Feeding-place مَطْعَم

Feel شعر u inf. شعور

Feeling عاطفة

Felicity سَعَادة

Fermented drink نَبيذ

Fertile خصب pc. 4

Fetters وِثاق

Few قليل, بعض a few of قليل

Few, to be قَلّ i

Fewness قِلّة

Fictitious فعَل pc. 8

Fidelity أمانة

Fiery ناري

Fifteen خمسة عشر

Fifth خامس

Fifty خمسون

Fight قتل 3 inf. قتال f. mutually 6

Figure صُورة pl. صُوَر

Figure, to صور 2 to f. to oneself 5

Fill, مُلْء

Fill, to ملأ a

Filosouf فَيْلَسُوف

Find وَجَدَ i inf. وِجدان f. out أنس 10 a thing

Fin de siècle = modern

Fine (of) جَيِّد, جليل, حسن poetry) رقيق (of weather) لطيف to think f. ظرف 10

Finger بَنان fem. f. tips أصْبع

Finish قضى i pass. 7

Fire نار fem.

Firm ثبت pc. حكم pc. pass. 4

Firm, to be ثَبَتَ u to make f. 2

Firmament سماء

Firman فرمان

Firmness حكم inf. 4

First أوَّل pl. أوائل adv. = acc.

First-fruits باكورة

Fish حُوت pl. حِيتان

Fit out, to هيّأ 2

Fitter أُوْلَى

Fitting, to be جَدُر u

Fixity دمج inf. 7

Flag لِواء pl. أَلْوية

Flagellator جَلَّاد

Flail (rod) قضيب

Flame لَهِيب to f. up 8

Flat سطح pc. pass. 2

Flavour طَعْم

Flee هَرَب u فرّ i

Fleet horse جَواد

Flesh بَشَر fleshly بشرى

Flight فرار

Fling نبذ i

Flood, to, intr. سيل i tr. 4

Flourish (نمو) نما u

Flow مَجْرى

Flow, to جَرَى i make to f. 4

Flower زَهَر pl. أزهار

Fly طير i

Foe = enemy

Fog ضَباب pl. ضَبابة

Fold طَوَى i

Folk قَوْم

Follow تَبِعَ a and 8 : f. out 3
f. up 8 following upon عَقِيب

Follower تابع pl. تَبَع, أتباع

Folly سَهْو

Food طَعام to beg f. of طعم
10 c. d. a.

Foodstuff رِزْق pl. أرزاق

Fool حمق elat.

Foot قَدَم pl. أَقْدام

Footpassenger راجِل

For, conj. إذْ, فإنّ prep. مِنْ أَجَل,
على, ل

Forbid حرم i and 2

Force قُوّة (of police) شِدّة

Force, to ضرّ 8 to f. the hand
of كره 4

Ford مَخاضة pl. مخاوض

Forehead جَبْهة

Foreigner أَعْجَمِيّ

Forenoon, to be in the ضحو 4

Forepart قدم pc. pass. 2

Forest غابة pl. reg.

Forestall درك 6

Forge فرى 8

Forget نَسِيَ a inf. نِسْيان to
make to f. 4

Forgetful نَسِيّ

Forgive (عفو) عفا u with عن

Forgiveness عَفْو

Form شَكْل, نَمَط pl. أشكال

Formation شكل 2 inf.

Formerly قبلا, قد (كان)

Forsake وَذَرَ a

Fort حِصْن pl. حصون

Fortify حصّن 2

Fortress قَلْعة pl. قلاع

Fortune حَظّ fortunately لِحُسْن الحظّ

Forty أربعون

Found, to أسّ 2

Four أَرْبَع

Fox تَعْلَب

Frame, to صنع a

Franc فرنك

France فرنسا

Franks, the الافرنج, الفرنج

Free, freeman حُرّ pl. أحرار f. (from) خلو pc. to set f. حرّ 2: to f. oneself خلص 5

Freedom حُرّية

French, Frenchman فَرَنْساوىّ

Frequently = many times

Fresh حدث pc.: = new

Fret جَزِعَ a

Friday يومر الجمعة, الجُمْعة

Fried in, to be صلى i

Friend صَديق, خَليل pl. أَصْدِقاء

Friendly وَدّى

Friendship مَحَبّة

Fright رَوْع

Frighten خوف 2 to be frightened روع 8

Frigid, to be ثلج 4

Frivolous, to be طيش i

From مِن, عَن

Front of, in أمام

Frozen جَمَد pc. جليد to be f. جمد u and 2

Fruit فكه pc. fem. ثَمَر pl. ثمار, to produce f. ثمر 4 ثمرات

Fry in صَلَى i c. d. a.

Fu-chun فوشان

Fuel حَطَب

Full مَلأَى dipt. fem. مَلْآن

Fun, to make لغا (لغو) u

Fundamental أساسىّ

Furnish جهز 2

Further, to عز وفر 2

Future قبل pc. 10: adj. pc. 4

Gabriel = Jibrīlu

Gain (profit) كَسْب

Gain (object) نيل a

Gambling قمار

Game لَعِب pl. ألعاب

Gaming قَمْر

Garden جَنَّة

Garlic ثُوم

Garrison حمى pc. fem.

Gate باب

Gather جنى i (souls) قَبَض i
g. in (harvest) حصل 2

Gehenna جَهَنَّم

General جنرال

General عَمّر pc. to become g.
عَمّر u

Generally على, غالبا, عُمُومًا,
العموم

Generalization عَمّر inf. 2

Generation, (men) of third ثوالث

Generosity مَكْرُمة pl. مكارم

Generous كَرِيم

Gentle لَطِيف to deal gently 5

Gentleman جنتلمان

Gentleness رِقّة

Genuine حقيقىّ

German ألمانى pl. ألمان

Germany المانيا

Get نيل a to get up (exhibition)
قوم 4

Gild موه 2

Girdle مِنْطَقة

Give عطو a وَهَب 4 c. d. a.

Give in, to وَهَن i

Gladden سرّ u gladness سُرُور

Gladstone غلادستون

Glance بَصَر pl. أبْصار

Glass زُجاج

Gloom كَدَر

Glorify سبح 2 (God) جلّ 4

Glorious جليل to be g. جلّ i

Glory عِزّة

Gluttony شَرَه

Go, go away ذَهَب a make to go
away 4: go back رجع i go
beyond عدو 5: go down ورد i
make to go down 4: go cheerfully نشط a go forth نفر i go
into (investigate) قضى 10: go
on قوم 10: go out خرج u inf.
خروج make to go out 4: go
round دور u go up صعد a علا
طَلَع u, (star) (علو) u inf.
طُلُوع go wide طيش i

Goad مِنْخَس

Goal غاية

Goat عَنْز

God اَللَّه a god إلاه

Gog = Jājūju

Gold ذَهَب

Goliath = Jālūtu

Good g. طَيِّب pc. صلح, خَيْر things خَيْرات

Good! good is... نِعْمَ

Good, to be u to do or make g. 4 حَسُنَ u صلح

Goodness حُسْن

Goodwill مُروءة

Gospel, the = al-'Injīlu

Govern حكم u

Government حُكومة pl. reg. دَوْلة

Governor حكم pc., pl. حُكّام his governorship (title) دولتلو

Grace مراحم pl. مرحمة

Grace, to show غوث 4 to ask for g. 10

Graceful ظريف

Gradual تدريجيّ

Grain حبّ coll. حَبّة

Grandfather جدّ pl. أَجْداد

Grant منح a (of Sultan) مدّ 4 inf. مَنْح

Grapes عِنَب

Grapnel مِخطاف

Grasp قبض i inf. قَبْض

Grass حشائش pl.

Gratify نعم 4

Gratuity صلة

Grave قَبْر

Grave, adj. رصين

Grayhaired شيب elat.

Gray hairs شَيْب

Great كَبير pl. كبار

Great, to become كَبُرَ u to be g. عزّ i to make g. 4

Greatness جُبْروت, عزّة his g. (title) عَزّتلو to attain g. = to be great

Greedy طَمّاع

Greeks, the = al-Rūmu

Green خضر adj. خُضْرة elat.

Greenness خضر inf. 9

Greens خُضَر

Grief غَمّ, أَسَف

Grievance مَساءة, سوء inf. 8

Grieve أَسَف a أَسِيَ a

Grievous case, to be in عَنِتَ a

Grind طحن a

Ground مَيْدان moist g. ثَرًى

Grow نُمُوّ u (نمو) نما inf. نَبَتَ u tr. 4

Grow up شبّ i

Grumble ذمر 5

Guard وَقَى i inf. وِقاية

Guest of, to become a ضيف i

Guidance هُدًى

Guide هَدَى i to be guided 8

Guided aright, to be رَشَدَ u to guide aright 4

Guinea جنيه

Gulp up لهم 8

Gush, inf. نَبْع

Habit مَلَكَة

Habitation مَسْكِن

Habitual عَادِىّ

Al-Hadi هدى pc.

Al-Hadyah الهدية

Haicheng های شنغ

Haifa حيفا

Hair شَعْر Hairdresser زين 2 pc.

Al-Hajjaj الحجاج

Half نِصْف Half-bow قاب

Halter زَمام

Hamasa حماسة

Al-Hamid الحامد

Hamidian حميدى

Hand يد fem. right h. يمين pl. أيمان on other h. = from other direction: to take in h. ولى 5

w.

Hand, to دَفَعَ a inf. دَفْع h. down, over سلم 2

Handicraft صناعة pl. صنائع

Handmill رَحًى fem.

Happen حَدَثَ u make to h. 4

Happy سعيد

Haram, the الحرم

Hard صُلْب

Hardened, to be (قسو) قسا u

Harm ضُرّ no h. لَا بَأْس

Harm, to ضرّ u

Harsh conduct مُقاساة

Harun هارون

Al-Hasan الحسن

Hashim هاشم

Haste سُرْعة

Hasten سرع 4

Hate, Hatred بُغْض

Haughty أَبِىّ

Haul قطر u

Hauran حوران

Have to, to ضرّ 8 pass. or = to see no escape from

Hayah حياة

Head رَأْس pl. رُؤُس (chief) رئيس

Headquarters = capital

Headstrongness جِماح

Heal بَرِئ 4

Health صِحّة

Healthy صحيح

Heap صُبْرة pl. reg.

Heaped up, to be رَكم 6

Hear سَمِعَ a inf. سَماع let hear
4: hearer pc.

Hearing, quick of سَمِيع

Heart قَلْب pl. قُلُوب

Heat حَرّ (of summer) قَيْظ

Heave (sigh) صَعِد 5

Heaven-s سَماء pl. سموات

Heavenly سماوّي

Heavy ثقيل to be h. ثَقُلَ u

Heed وَعَى i heedful, pc.

Height=elevation: (hill) رَبْوة pl.
reg. utmost h. جُهْد

Hell = the burning

Help إِسْعاف

Help, to سعد 3 : نَصَر u inf. نَصْر

Herb عُشْب pl. أعشاب

Herbage كَلأ ,ربيع pl. رباع

Herd (a crowd) جَماعة

Herd, to رَعَى a

Here هُهْنَا

Here I am ها انا ذا Here he is
هو ذا

Hero بَطَل

Herzegovina الهرسك

Hesitate أخر 5

Hew نحت i

Hewer of millstones نقّار

Hide, tr. كَنّ 4 خفى 4

Hideous, to render شوه 2

Hidingplace مَخْبَأة

High علو pc. most High pf. 6

Hijaz, the الحجاز

Hijrah, adj. هجرّي

Hilani هيلانى

Hill تَلّ pl. تِلال

Hind هِنْدُ

Hinder منع a

Hint at, to عرض ب 2

Hire أُجْرة ,أَجْر

Hire, to أجر 10

History أرخ inf. 2 historical
— ى

Hit صوب 4

Hold مسك 4 lay hold of 5

Homeland وَطَن

Homogeneous جنس pc. 6

Honein = Ḥunainun

Honour شَرَف ,عِرْض

Honour, to كرم 2 : (persons) 4

Honourable شريف

147

Honoured (person) = generous

Hope, n. ثقة ,رَجاء ,أَمَل

Hope, hope for أمل رَجا (رجو) u

Horizon أُفْق

Horn قَرْن

Horrible فظيع

Horse جَواد (noble) ,حِصان ,coll. خَيْل

Horsemanship فُروسيّة

Hospital شفى pc. pass. 10

Hostile عدو pc. 3

Hot حارّ

Hotel فُنْدُق

Hotness حَرارة

Hour ساعة pl. reg.

House مَنْزِل ,بَيْت pl. بُيوت

Household أَهْل pl. reg.

How? كَيْف How much, many, long كَمْ

However مَهْما كان ,ولقد ,وإن

Humaid حميد

Humanity إنسانيّة

Humble حَقير

Humble, to حقر 4 to think h. 8 and 10: to be humbled خَشَعَ a

Humiliation خُشوع

Humorous فُكاهىّ

Humour, see ill h.

Humpbacked حدب elat. to be h. 12

Hundred مائة pl. مئات

Hundredweight قنْطار whole h.s قناطير مُقَنْطَرة (Kor. 3, 12)

Hungarians, the المَجَر

Hunger جُوع

Hungry جُوع pc.

Hunt, to صيد i and 8: hunter, pc. 1

Hurl قذف i

Hurry عَجَل ,عجلة to be in a h. عَجِلَ a to hurry 2: to ask to be hurried 10

Hurt وجع 2 ألم 4

Husband زَوْج

Hyacinth (stone) ياقوت

Hypocritical, to be نفق 3: hypocrite, pc.

I أَنا

Iblis = 'Iblīsu

Ice جليد

Idea فِكْرة ,مَعْنًى

Identify دمج : pass. 7

Idrīs = 'Idrīsu

10—2

If إِنْ, لَوْ, إِذَا if that أَنْ, لو

Ignoble دنى

Ignorance جَهالة, جَهْل the I.
الجاهليّة

Ignorant, to be جَهِلَ a ignorant,
pc. pl. جُهَلاء

Ill (bad) سَيِّء Ill is... بِئْسَ

Ill humour ضَجَر

Ill-luck نَحْس

Illness عِلّة

Illumine نور 2

Ill will سوء

Al-'Imad العِماد

Imaginary وَهْمِيّ

Imagine = figure to oneself:
Imagination = inf.

Imam إِمام

Imbibe كرع 2

Imitate قلد 2 imitation, inf.
imitator, pc.

Immediately للحال

Immense = in large quantity

Impatience ضُجْرة

Imperial استعماري, مُلوكِيّ

Implement أداة pl. أَدوات

Importance أَهَمِّيّة

Important هَمّ pc. 4 to be i. 4

Impossible, to be عذر 5

Impress أثر 2 impression, inf.
to be impressed 5

Imprison حَبَسَ i pass. 7

Impure خبيث

In إِذ in ب, فى inasmuch as in
that حَيْث

Inauspicious شأم elat.

Incapable عجز pc.

Incarcerate سَجَنَ u

Inception صَدْر

Inch قيراط pl. قراريط

Incident حدث pc. fem.

Incite حثّ u

Inciting, Incitement بعث pc.
pl. بواعث

Incline ميل i inclination, inf.
مَيْل pl. أميال make to incline
to one 10

Income دَخْل

Increase زيادة

Increase, tr. زيد i c. d. a. intr. 8

Incumbent on, to be وجب على i

Incursion غارة pl. reg.

Indeed لَ or energetic of vbs.

Independent, to be قلّ 10

India = al-Hindu

Indian هندى pl. هنود

Indicate دلّ على u

Indication of دليل على

Individual فَرْد pl. أفراد

Indulgence رفْق

Inevitable وقع pc.

Inferior دنىّ elat.

Infidel لحد pc. 4

Influence = impression : نُفوذ

Inform خبر 4 with ب well informed خبير to be informed, to get information وقف على i

Ingenuity مَهارة

Inhabitant سكن pc. pl. سُكّان

Inherit وَرِثَ i

Initiative جهِد inf. 8

Injury أذى, عَطْب

Ink مداد

Inkhorn محبرة

Innocent بَرِيء to declare i. بَرِئ 2

Inquire بَحْث a inf.

Inscribe رقم u

Inscription كتابة

Inside دخل pc.

Insight بصيرة

Insignificant قَزِم

Insist لحّ 4

Insolent, to be طغى a

Instead of دُون

Instigate حمل i

Instinct ذَكاء فطْرِيّ

Institution نظام pl. ات

Instrument آلة pl. reg.

Insure ضَمِنَ a

Insurrection ثَوْرة

Intellect عَقْل

Intellectual عقلىّ

Intelligent عقل pc. pl. عُقَلاء

Intend رود 4

Intention نِيّة pl. نوايا

Inter دسّ u

Intercede شَفَعَ a

Intercessor شَفيع

Interconnected وصل 6 pc.

Intercourse عِشْرة

Interdict حرم 2

Interest (usury) رِبًا to earn i. مَصْلَحة (advantage)(ربو)ربا u, هَمّ (care) inf. 8 فائدة

Interested, to be هَمّ 8

Interesting هَمّ pc. 4

Interfere دخل 3

Interior سَريرة

Internal داخلىّ

Interval خلال

Intervene حَول u

Intervention مُداخَلة

Interview = visit : (reporter) = talk to

Intimate جليس

Into فى ,إلَى

Intoxicant سكر pc. 4 fem.

Intrenchment مَعْقل

Introduce (practice) بدع 8

Intruder دخيل

Intuition لسان الحال

Invalid عليل

Invalidated, to be نقض 8

Invective بُهْتان

Inventor بدع pc. 8

Invert قلب 2

Invigorate نعش 2 and 4

Invite (دعو) دعا u

Inward بطن pc.

Al-Irak العراق

Iranian إيرانى

Irdab اردبّ

Irem = 'Iramu

Iron حَديد adj. حديدىّ

Irreproachable = there did not take him a blaming of a blamer

Irrigate روى 4

Irrigation أمر الرى ,الرَىّ

Isaac = Isḥāqa (gen.)

Ishmael = 'Ismāʻīlu

Islam = al-'Islāmu

Islamic إسلامىّ

Island جزيرة

Isolation وَحْدة

Israel إسرائيل

Italian إيطالىّ

Italy ايطاليا

Item خَصْلة pl. خِصال

Jaafar جعْفر

Jacob = Yaʻqūba (gen.)

Jaffa يافا

Al-Jahiz الجاحظ

Jap يابانىّ pl. reg.

Jeer at هكمـ ب 5

Jemal ed Din جمال الدين

Jerusalem = al-Qudsu

Jesus عيسَى

Jeved جواد

Jews, the = al-Yahūdu

Jiddah جُدّة

Jilliq جلّق

Jinn جنون pl.

Job = 'Aiyūbu

John يَحْيَى

Join وَصَلَ i to j. together بشر 6

Joseph = Yūsufu

Journal دَفْتَر

Journey سَفَر, pl. سفرات

Journey, to سفر 3

Joy فَرَح

Judge قضى pc.

Judgment حُكْم

Judicial قضائيّ

Jug إِبْرِيق

Juggler شعوذ pc.

July يوليه

Junction لقى pc. pass. 8

June يونيه

Juridical فِقْهِيّ

Justice عَدْل

Justify زكو 2

Kaab كَعْب

Al-Kadam القدم

Kadi = judge : the Grand K. = the K.

Kāi-yuen كاى يوين

Kan قان

Al-Karak • الكرك

Kasr ed Dubarah قصر الدوبارة

Kasr-el-Nil قصر النيل

Kata قطاة

Katar قطر

Kazim كاظم

Keen حَدِيد

Keen-sighted بَصِير to be k. بَصُرَ u

Keep صون 8 : حفظ ب k. safe inf. صيانة to k. on = continue : to k. (secret) = conceal

Al-Khaizuran الخيزران

Khalid خالد

Khalif خليفة pl. خُلَفاء

Kharbin خاربين

Al-Khattab الخطاب

Khedive, Khedivial خُدَيْوِيّ pl. reg.

Kiblah قبلة adj. قبلى

Kick رفس i

Kill قَتَل u inf. قَتْل

Kilometre كيلومتر pl. ات

Kind جنس pl. أَجْناس

Kindle وقد 4 شعل a

Kindler وقّاد

Kindliness رَأفة

Kindness عرف pc. pass.

King مَلِك pl. مُلُوك

Kingdom مَمْلَكَة

Kinship قُرْبَى

Kirin كيرين

Kirman كرمان

Kisra كسرى

Al-Kiswah الكسوة

Kitchen مَطْبَخ

Knight فرس pc.

Knock (door) قرع a

Knot, to عَقَد i inf. عَقْد

Know (connaître) عرف i (savoir)
عرف i to make k. عَلِمَ a دَرَى
2: not to k. نكر 4: knowing
that علْمًا ان to be known to
عرف ب 5

Knowledge مَعْرِفة

Koran, the = al-Qur'ānu

Koreish = Coreish

Kufic كوفىّ

Kuweit الكويت

Labourer عمل pc. pl. عَمَلَة

Lad غُلام

Lame عرج elat.

Lament, inf. نَدْب

Lamp مَنارة l. stand قِنْدِيل

Land طين pl. أَرْض pl. أَراضٍ: Land
بَرّ (opp. to sea) :أَطيان

Landmark معلم

Landowners أرباب الأَطيان

Language لُغة, لَهْجة pl. reg.

Large = great

Lash جَلَد i

Last أَخِير adj. آخر lastly, acc.

Latchet سَيْر pl. سُيُور

Late (dead) رحم pc. pass.: of
late = recently

Latter life, the الآخِرة

Laud ثنى على 4

Laudation ثَناء

Laugh ضَحِك a make to l. 4

Laughter = inf. ضَحِك

Lavish بذل i u l. praise on
طرو 4

Lawful حَلال

Lawful, to be حَلّ i to declare
l. 2: to make l. 4

Lawsuit دَعْوَى

Lay aside همل 4

Layer طَبَقَة

Lead رَصاص

Lead, to قود u (road) فضى 4:
to l. out زَفّ u to l. to (result)
أَدَى 2: take the l. = take in
hand

Leader زَعِيم pl. زُعَماء

Leaf وَرَقَة pl. أَوْراق

Leap وُثوب i inf. وثب

Learn علم 5 learned, pc.

Learned (the) عالِم pl. عُلَماء

Least, at the على الأَقَلّ

Leather-carpet نطَع

Leave (depart) صَرف 7 (a place)
تَرَك u inf. to l. alone برح a
تَرَك

Lebanon لُبْنان

Leg ساق pl. سُوق

Legal شَرْعِيّ

Legion of Honour اللجياون دونور

Legislative Council
مجلس شُورَى القوانين

Lend قرض 4 عار 4 c. d. a.

Length طُول

Lengthy طويل

Lenient, to be دهن 4

Lentils عَدَس

Less اقلّ

Less, to make, to lessen قلّ 2
and 4

Lest (مخافة) أن

Let وَدَع a not to let = hinder:
let alone يَذَرُ, وَذَرُ let down
نزل 4 let us لِ and apoc.

Letter (of alphabet) حَرْف pl.
حُروف (epistle) كتاب pl.
كُتُب (opp. of spirit) حرفيَّة

Level عدل to be on a level
سوى 8

Liable قبل pc.

Liau-yang لياوينغ

Liberality كَرَم

Library مَكْتَبة

Lie (on the ground) om. (tell a
lie) كَذَب i to call one a liar 2

Life حياة, حيوة Lifetime عُمْر
by the life of لَعَمْرُ to prolong
life to in عمر 2 to wish long
life to حيّ 2

Light (opp. of darkness) نور
(of lamp) ضَوْء to be l. نور u
to l., l. up ضوء 4

Light (opp. of heavy) خفيف to
be l. خفّ i to make l. (easy)
2: to make l. of 10

Lightning بَرْق adj. برقيّ

Like شِبْه, مِثْل, ك pl. أمثال

Like, adj. شبيه

Like, to = to be satisfied with:
Would you like? هل لك فى

Liken شبه 2 to be like each
other 6

Likewise, like that كذلك

Limit حَدّ pl. حُدود

Limpid صفو pc.

Line خَطّ (of poetry) = verse : (of writing) سَطْر pl. سُطور to take a (particular) line سلَك مَسْلَك u

Linger = remain

Listen سمع a listener, pc. 8

Literature أدَب pl. آداب

Litigation خُصومة

Little = small or few : l. is ما قلّ

Littleness قلّة

Live حَيِيَ, حیّ a to make l. 4 to let l. 10 living حَیّ

Livelihood معيشة to gain a l. عيش i

Lo إذا

Load وزْر to carry (a load) وزر i loadcarrying, pc.

Load, to حمل 2

Loadstone مغناطيس

Loan قَرْض

Loathe سَئِمَ a inf. سأم

Locomotive وابور pl. وبورات

Lodge (oneself) أوَى i tr. 4

Loftiness سُمُوّ

Lofty سمو pc. (building) شهق pc. (hill) شمخ pc.

Lokman = Luqmānu

London لوندره

Long طويل as l. as ما, ما دام ere long = in the near, the coming

Long, long for, to شوق 8

Long, to be طول u to make l. 4

Longing شَوْق

Look نَظَر pl. أنظار

Look, look at نظر u looker, pc. to l. after (a thing) قوم ب u to l. (upon) عبر 8 inf. قيام

Loose حلّ u فكّ u

Lord (master) رَبّ pl. أرباب (title) اللورد

Lose خَسِرَ a l. faith in قنط من a l. no time بدر 3

Loss خَسارة

Lost, to be ضيع i to let be l. 2

Lot = Lūtun

Love حُبّ, مَحَبّة

Love, to حبّ 4 and 10 inf. حُبّ

Lover عشق pc. pl. عُشّاق

Low سفل, واطئ pc. : lowest part, elat.

Lower, to حطّ u غضّ من u

Lowly, to be خَشَعَ *a*

Loyalty خلص inf. 4

de luxe فخر pc. pass. 8

Maan مَعْن

Macedonia مقدونيا

Madman جنّ pc. pass.

Madness جُنُون

Magazine (book) مَجَلّة pl. reg.
مَخْزَن (store) دفتر

Magnitude عَظَمَة

Magog = Mājūju

Mahdi هدى pc. pass.

Mahmil محمل

Mahmud محمود

Mail بريد

Mainly بالأكثر

Maize ذُرة

Majesty = excellency

Makariyus مقاريوس

Make صَنْع

Make, to جَعَلَ *a* (appoint) عين
2: (poetry) = say : m. for قصد
i m. to (do a thing) همّر ب *u*
m. way خلو سبيل 2

Maker (of poetry) = sayer

Malik مالك

Mameluke مملوك

Al-Mamun المأمون

Man المَرْء c. art. امْرُؤ, الإِنْسَان
a man رَجُل pl. رِجَال men ناس

Manage دبر 2 management, inf.

Manchuria منشوريا

Manhood مُرُوءة

Manifest بدو 4

Manifold كثر pc. 6

Mankind = the flesh

Manliness رُجُولِيّة

Manner نَمَط

Manners آداب pl.

Manufacture وجد 4

Many رُبَّ كثير pl. كِثَار many a
how many a كَأَيِّنْ مِن

Map خريطة pl. خرائط

March (of army) زَحْف (month)
مارس

March, to زَحَفَ *a*

Mare فَرَس

Margin شَطّ

Mark ears of cattle بتك 2

Market سُوق pl. أسواق

Marriage زَواج

Marry زوج 2 c. d. a.

Marvellous فَرِيّ

Marwan مَروانُ

Mary = Maryama (gen.)

Marzuban مرزبان

Mass جُلّ (of people) سَواد

Massacre = slaughter

Massacre, to قتل 2

Mast صرى pc.

Master صاحِب pl. أَصحاب be- come m. حوذ 10 reg.: get mastery of غلب 5

Masterful ذو شدّة, جبّار (owner of force)

Mate قرين

Material مادّة pl. موادّ adj. مادّىّ

Matter شأن, أمْر pl. شُؤُن

Mature درك 4

Al-Mausil المَوصل

May (month) مايو, أيّار

May, vb. مكن من 5: = to be permitted: قَدْ طوع 10 with impf.

Meadow غُوطة pl. غيطان

Meal طُعْمة

Mean (not extreme) وسطٌ elat. بُخَلاء .pl (greedy) بخيل

Mean, to = to want

Meaning مَعْنًى

Means وسائل, واسطة pl. by m. of بِواسطة by no m. = not at all

Measure مكْيال to give by m. كَيل i to take by m. 8: to give short m. طفّ 2

Measurement مساحة

Meat لَحْم

Mecca = Makkatu

Mechanic ميكانيكى

Mediation وسط inf. 5

Medicine دَواء

Medina = al-Madīnatu: of M. مَدَنِىّ

Meekness وَداعة

Meet لقَىَ a and 3 قبل 3: (wishes) وفق 4: m. together لقى 8: صدف m. with 3

Meeting-place معهد

Melancholy, adj. سجو pc.

Melt ذوب u

Member عُضْو pl. أعضاء

Menace هدّ inf. 2: to m. وعد 4

Mention ذِكْر

Mention, to ذَكَر u not to m. فضلا عن

Merchandise = traffic متجر pl.

Merchant تجر pc. pl. تُجّار

Merchant, adj. تِجارِيّ

Merciful رَحِيم

Mercy رَحْمة have m. = pity

Merely ل with جرد pc. pass. 2

Merv مَرو

Merwah, the = al-Marwatu

Message رسالة

Metonymy كِناية

Metre (in poetry) وَزن (measure of length) متر pl. أَمتار

Michael = Mīkālu

Midday prayer ظُهر

Middle (of time) نِصف pc. pass. 8

Midian = Madyanu

Midmost وَسَط

Mien طَلْعة

Might, vb. قَد with impf.

Mighty عَظِيم pl. عُظَماء to be m. عَظُم

Mild لطيف

Mildness لَطافة

Military عسكرى

Mill طاحون

Million مليون

Mind خاطِر, فُؤَاد

Mine مَنْجَم (coal) مَعْدِن

Mingle مزج 8 mingled, pc. pass. 1

Minister (delegate) عمد pc. pass. 8

Minute دقيقة

Miracle عجز fem. pc. 4, pl. reg.

Mirror مِرْآة

Miscellany مجموعة

Mischief, to make نزع a شغب 3

Miserable, to be شَقِيَ a

Misery شَقاء

Misfortune حدث pc. fem.

Mislead غوى 4

Miss (aim) خطئ 4 (to lose) فقد i

Mission = message

Mistaken, to be = to miss (aim)

Mr. المستر

Mistress ذات pl. ذوات

Mithkal مثقال

Mitre = turban

Mix, tr. خَلَطَ to m. with 3 intr. 8

Moayyad = Muaiyad

Mock at سَخِرَمِن a

Model شاكلة

Modern عَصْرِيّ

Modesty حىّ, حَياء inf. 10

Mohammad = Muḥammadun

Mohammadan = Islamic

Mohammadanism = Islam

Moisture رُطوبة

Molest أَذى 4

Money مال pl. أَمْوال

Monopolize attention شَغَل a

Monsieur المسيو

Month شَهْر pl. أَشْهُر

Moon قَمَر

Moor مَغْرِبى

Moorish = Moroccan

Moral مَغْزًى

Moral = educational

Moralist أُدب pc. 5

More كثر elat. وفر elat. still
    بالأكثر more

Moreover = along with that

Morning صَباح to be (do) in the
    m. صبح 4 : early m. سَحَر to
    go out in the m. (غدو) غدا u
    m. and evening صَباح مَساء

Moroccan = مَرّاكشى

Morocco مَرّاكُش,
    المغرب الاقصى

to-Morrow غَدًّا

Mortar up, to شيد 2

Moses see Musa

Moslem سلم pc. 4 : to become a
    M. 4

Moslem, adj. = Islamic

Mosque مَسْجِد, جامع

Most, at the فى الأكثر mostly
    = usually

Mote قَذًى

Mother أُمّ

Motion حَرَكة pl. reg.

Mould (nature) فطْرة pl. فطَر

Mound كُومة pl. أكوام

Mountain جَبَل pl. جبال

Mountain, adj. جبالى, جبلى

Mouse فارة

Mouth فُوه pl. أفواه

Move, intr. حرك 5 : move round
    and round حول عن 5

Movement = motion : (political)
    فتْنة

Muaiyad مؤيّد

Muawiya معاوية

Much كَثير adv. = acc. to be m.
    كَثُر u to make m. 4 : to desire
    m. 10

Muchness كَثْرة

Mud وَحَل pl. أوحال

Mufti فتو pc. 4 : the Grand M.
    = the M. or the m. of the
    Egyptian dwellings

Al-Muhallab المهلب

Mukden موكدن

Mule بَغْل pl. بغال

Munificence سَخاء

Murghab, the المرغاب

Musa موسى

Music الموسيقى

Muslim = Moslem

Must = there is no escape that, *or* I do not see an escape from

Mustaches شوارب pl.

Al-Mustansir المستنصر

Mustard خَرْدَل

Mutter همس, دمدم i

Al-Muweilihi المويلحى

Myrrh مُرّ

Nail مِسْمار

Name اِسْم pl. أسماء

Name, to سمو 2

Namesake سَمِىّ

Nap رَقْدة

Napoleon نابوليون

Narrate روى i

Narrative خَبَر pl. أخبار

Narrow ضَيِّق

Narrow, to, intr. ضيق i : tr. 2

Naskh نسخ

Nation أُمّة

Native = patriotic

Nature ماهية, طَبيعة natural طبيعى naturally أنّ بديهى

Naught, to come to زول u

Nay بَل

Near قَريب, على مَقْربة من nearer دنِّى elat.

Near, to دنو 3: to be n. قُرْب inf. قُرْب to bring near 2: to draw n. gradually 6: to get n. 8

Nearly كود a

Nearness قُرْب

Necessarily so = upon it

Necessary, to be لزِم i وجب a necessary, pc.: n. things لوازم pl.

Necessitate لزِم 4 c. d. a. قضى 8 to n. to oneself لزِم 8

Necessity = no escape: upon necessity عند اللزوم

Need حاجة pl. reg. be in n. of = have n. unto

Needy حوج pc. 8

Neglect همل 4

Neglected (of composition) مُرْسَل

Negligent, to be غفَل u negligent, pc.

Negociations, to enter into دخل 6

Neighbour جار pl. جيران

Neighbourhood = nearness

Neighbouring جور pc. 3

Nejd نجد

Nephew = brother's son

Nervous, to be فَزِعَ a

Nest وُكْنة pl. reg.

Never لَنْ : not...ever

Nevertheless = along with all that

New جديد

News نَبَأ pl. أنباء to tell n. حدث 2

Newspaper جريدة

New York نيو يورك

Next, adv. ثُمَّ

Next to, to be ولى i

Next world = latter life

Nice طَيِّب to be n. طيب i

Niggardly, to be بَخِلَ a

Nigh, to bring زلف 4

Nigher to أولى ب

Night لَيْلة pl. لَيْل by n. لَيْلًا to pass the n. بيت i

Nile, the النيل

Ninety تِسْعون

No ليس, لا, ما

Noah = Nūḥun

Nobility شَرَف

Noble شريف, كريم pl. أشراف (descent) عريق fem. شريفات

Nobleness نَباهة

Nolens volens طَوْعًا او كَرْهًا, طوعا وكرها

Nomad life بَداوة

Noon ظُهْر

North شمال northwards, acc.

Northern شمالى

Not لا, ما, لم (it will not be that) لَنْ

Notable نبغ pc.

Notably = and especially

Note, to = to see

Notebook دفتر

Nothing, come to لشى 6

Notice, to ثَقَفَ a

Notify اذن 4

Nourishment قُوت

Novel رواية pl. reg.

November نوفمبر

Now الآن, ف, و now...now تارة... تارة now and then أحيانا, فى بعض الأحيان

Number عَدَد pl. أَعْداد numerous, pc. 5

Number, to حصى 4

Nutriment غذاء

Nutritive غذائى

O يا O you there = O this

Oath يمين pl. أَيْمان to take o. حلف i mutually 6

Obedience طاعة

Obedient, to be قنت u

Obey طوع 4

Object خُطْب, غَرَض, قَصْد o. in view مقصود

Object to, to رَغِبَ عن a

Objurgate قسم 4

Obligatoriness لزم inf. 8

Obliterate طمس i

Obscure ستر Obscurity عمى inf. 2

Observation عبر inf. 8

Observe رعى inf. رِعاية, (follow) قوم 4

Obstacle منع pc.

Obstruct حدّ 3

Obtain = be to him

Obviate درك 6

Occasion حِين

Occasionally من حين الى حين (اخر)

Occupy ولى 5 (office, attention) حلّ a (country) شغل 8 Occupation, inf.

Occur خطر i 8 (to mind) وفق and u

Occurrence وُجود

October اكتوبر

Ode قصيدة

Of من is frequently used in modern Arabic instead of the classical constr. and gen.

Offer عرض i 2 قدم (opinion)

Office مَنْصِب

Officer ضبط pc., pl. ضبّاط

Official وظف pc. pass. 2

Official, adj. رَسْمى

Offspring سُلالة

Often مِرارًا as o. as كُلَّما

Oftentimes كثيرًا ما

Og عوج

Oil دُهْن

Oilseller = Zaiyat

Old قديم of old = acc.: o. man شَيخ

Oman عمان

Omar = 'Umaru

162

Omen طير pc. to draw ill o. 5

Once مَرّة at o. = immediately

One واحِد ,أَحَد one of بَعْض
one...other بعض...بعض one
day, etc. ذاتَ يَوْمٍ

Oneiza عنيزة

Oneness وحد inf. 8

Onions بَصَل

Only فَقَطْ, إنَّما or = not...ex-
cept: only that غَيْرَ أَنْ,
على أَنْ

Open (the) حَوْمة o. ground
فَضاء

Open, to فتح a

Operation عملِيّة

Opine = see good

Opinion رَأْي in the o. of عِنْدَ

Opportunity فُرْصة pl. فُرَص

Oppose oneself عرض 5

Opposite عَكْس

Opposition مُعارضة to show o.
رَدّ 5

Oppression جَوْر oppressive, pc.

Option خير inf. 8 optional
اختياري

Or او أَمْ, أَوْ or else with subj.

Ordain سنّ u

Order نظام to keep o., inf. نَظُمْ
in o. to, that كى ,ل

Order, to أَمَرَ ب u

Organization نظم inf. 2

Oriental شَرْقِي

Origin أَصْل

Original أصلي

Originally = in the origin

Originate نشأ a tr. 4

Orion الجَوْزاء

Ornament زينة

Ornament, to زين 2 : to be
ornamented 8

Orphan يتيم pl. يَتامَى

Orphanhood يُتْم

Orthodox أَصيل (pure)

Other سوَى or غَيْر, آخَر o. than
in o. words أَيْ the o. = the
rest of سائر others = other
than he, etc.

Otherwise = and if not

Othman = ʿUthmānu : Ottoman
عثماني

Outcry هتاف to make o. هتف i

Outrage = dangerous event

Outside خارِج, ظاهِر

Outward ظاهِر o. journey ذَهاب

Oven تَنُّور

Over على, إلى

Overcome قَهَر a

Overflow طفح a فيض i make to o. 4

Overhear = hear

Override عرض 3

Overtake درك 4

Overturn قلب inf. 7

Own, pron. om. or add بالذات to suff.

Own, to مَلَك i or = to have

Owner ذو, صحب pc. pl. اولو

Ox ثَوْر pl. بَقَر

Pacific = peaceful

Page صحيفة, صَفْحة pl. صُحُف

Pain = hurt

Pains (trouble) سَعْى to take p. 8 عنى

Paint نقش u inf. نَقْش painter نقّاش

Palace بَلاط

Palatable عَذْب

Palm (of hand) كَفّ pl. أَكُفّ

Palm (of hand) نَخْلة pl. coll., palmgrove نَخِيل

Panada ثَرِيد

Panegyric طرى inf. 4

Pangs (of hunger) ضَوْر

Panic stricken, to be جفل 4

Panther فَهْد

Paper قِرْطاس

Pardon, to give غَفَر i to ask p. 10

Parents ولد pc. أَب du.

Paris باريس

Parliament برلمان, مجلس نيابى

Parliamentary نيابى

Part (fraction) بَعْض (division) قِسْم (opp. of whole) = portions: for my part = from my direction: on the part of (people) من عند

Part, to فرق 5

Participate = be partner

Particle شَذَر pl. reg. fem.

Particular خصّ elat.

Particularity خصّ pc. fem. pl. خواصّ

Particularize خصّ 2, pass. 8

Particularly على, خُصوصاً الخصوص

Parting فِراق

Partner شَريك to be p. with
شرك 3: to make p. 4

Party (political) حِزْب

Pasha باشا pl. باشاوات

Pass مُرور inf. مرّ ب, على u فوت
(a place) جوز 3: p. away مضى i
inf. مضيّ p. by فوت, inf.
p. on جوز 3: p. over into فوات
5 حول

Passenger رُكّاب pc. pl. ركب
سفر pc. 3

Passion هَوًى

Past مضى pc.

Pasture مَرْعًى p. ground رَبْع
pl. رُبوع

Path مسالك pl. سَبيل

Patience صَبْر to have p. صَبَر i

Patient صبر pc.

Patriarch = chief of fathers

Patriotic (national) وَطَنِيّ

Patriotism وطنيّة

Patron مَوْلًى, وَلِيّ

Pay رواتب pl.

Pay, to (of a business) رَبِحَ a
tr. أدى 2, inf. أَداء: to p. in
advance سلف 4: to p. in full
وفى 2

Peace سَلام to make p. with
صلح 3: to make p. with one
another 8

Peaceful سِلْمِيّ

Peaceful, to be هدأ a سكن u

Pearl دُرّة coll. لُؤْلُؤ

Peer = look

Pelt رشق u

Pen قَلَم

Penetration = subduing

Peninsula = island

People أهال pl. أَهْل

Perceive درك 4: = feel, be
sensible of

Perchance لَعَلّ

Perdition هَلاك

Perfect, to be كَمِل i تمّ u, a
perfect, pc.: to perfect, 4

Perform صنع a performance
inf. 8

Perhaps رُبَّما

Period عَهْد

Periodical دفتر

Perish, to هلك i to cause to p.
4: to make to p. ضيع 4

Permitted, to be جوز u permissible, pc.: to permit 4

Perpetual, to be خلد u to per-
petuate 2

Persepolis	إِصْطَخُر
Persevere	3 ثبر
Persians	فُرْس
Persist	4 صرّ
Person	شَخْص pl. أشخاص
Personal	شخصى
Personality	ذات
Perspicuous	بين pc. 4
Pervert	i فَتَنَ
Petrify	5 حجر
Phantom	طَيْف
Pharaoh	= Fir'aunu
Pharisee	فارسى
Phase	مَظْهَر
Philosopher	فَيْلَسُوف
Philosophize, to	فلسف 2
Philosophy	فَلْسَفة
Physician	طبيب pl. أطِبّاء
Piano	بيانو
Piastre	قِرْش
Pickaxe	مِعْوَل
Pick up	لقط 8
Picnic	نزه 5
Piece	قِطْعة pl. قِطَع
Pierce (bullet)	نفذ u
Piety	بِرّ
Pile up	شيد i

Pilgrim	حَجّ pc. pl. حُجّاج
Pillage	نَهْب inf.
Pillar	عَمُود
Pine	وَجْد a inf. وَجِدَ
Pious	وَرِع to be p. بَرّ u
Pitch (tent)	نَصَبَ u
Pitiful	شجِيّ
Pity	رَحْمة with ب
Pity, to	رَحِمَ a
Place	موضع, مَحَلّ pl. مِحالّ, مَكان pl. أَمْكِنة, أماكن
Place, to	وَضَعَ a
Plague	وباء pl. أوْبِئة
Plain (level ground)	سَهْل, ساحة
Plain speaking	صرح inf. 2
Plan	طريقة
Plan, to	دبر 5
Plantation	بُسْتان
Play	لَعْب player, pc. pl. reg.
Play, to	لَعِبَ a
Playground	مَلْعَب
Pleasant	لذيذ
Pleasantness	حُبُور
Please, to	عجب 4 : would you please هل لك فى
Pleasure	كَيْف, لَذّة to find p. لذّ 8

Plentiful وفر pc. 5

Plenty خِصْب

Plot, to كَيْد i inf. كيد

Pluck up جثّ 8

Plunder غنيمة

Plunder, to سلَب u inf. سُلْب

Pocket جَيْب

Poet شاعر pl. شُعَراء

Poetry شعْر poetic شعرى

Point نُقْطة p. of view جِهَة, جهة نَظَر

Point, to دلّ u to p. to شور الى 4

Poison سُمّ pl. سموم

Police بوليس

Polish هذب inf. 2

Political, Politician سِياسيّ pl. reg.

Politics, Policy سِياسة

Poll-tax خَراج

Ponder = to plan

Pony مُهْر pl. مِهار

Poor فَقير (wretched) مِسْكين

Pope بابا pl. باباوات pr. n. بوب

Popular أهلى

Port Arthur بور آرثر

Portion جُزْء pl. أجزاء

Position موقع, مَرْكَز, مَنْزِلة to be in a p. to اتى 5

Possessed of ذو, ذات

Possession of, to put in مكن من 2: reflex. 5

Possible, to be مكن 4: possibility, inf.: as much as p. على قَدْر الإمكان

Post (letter) بوسطة (an office) = office

Postponement, to ask for نظر 10

Pour صبّ u (tears) سيل i to pour itself out هيل 7

Poverty فَقْر reduce to poverty 4

Power دَوْلة pl. دُوَل (nation) قُوّة

Powerful قدير

Practical فَعّال

Practice = works = أعمال

Praise (God) حَمْد (man) مَدْح praise to (God) سُبْحان

Praise, to حَمِدَ a

Praiseworthy, object of praise مدح pc. pass.

Pray, say prayers صلو 2

Prayer صَلَوة, pl. reg. (informal) دُعاء

Precede سبق i

Precincts = circle

Preeminence بَراعة

Prefecture إمارة

Prefer فضل 2 أثر 4

Prejudice حقد pl. أحقاد

Prepare عدّ 4 to make preparations 10

Prepared حضر pc.

Preponderate رجح (alternately) 5

Prescribe = enjoin

Presence حَضْرة

Present (time), the الحال

Present at, with, to be حَضَر u to p. (a person, thing) 4: to p. oneself شَخَص a (to offer) 4 هدى وجد :(give) 4

Present, adj. حضر pc.: at p. = in the p. time: (opp. of late) حالِيّ

Preserve حَفظ a inf. حفظ preserver, pc. pl. حُفّاظ p. carefully 3: ask to p. 10

President = chief

Press (newspaper) صحافة

Press, to عصر i

Pressure شدّ inf. 2

Prevail قدر i

Prevent منع a inf. مَنْع

Previous سبق pc.

Price ثَمَن

Pride كِبْرِياء

Primitive = first

Principal (chief) علىّ

Principle مَبْدَأ

Prison سِجْن

Private (life) خُصُوصِيّ private persons خاصّة

Privilege ميز inf. 8 pl. fem. privileged, pc.

Probable = perhaps

Probably على المحتمَل

to Proceed أمّا بَعْدُ

Process (of time) مدى inf. 6

Proclaim نشر u

Produce صنع pc. pass. fem.

Produce, to خرج 4

Product حصل pc. pass., pl. fem.

Profess (a religion) دين ب

Professor أُسْتاذ pl. أساتذة

Proffer قدم 2 with إلى

Proficient, to be فوق u

Profit رِبْح

Programme بروجرام

Progress, to رقى 8: progress, inf. to make to p. 2

Prohibit نَهَى a

Prohibition = bound

Prolonged, to be = to be long

Promise وَعْد

Promise, to وَعَد i

Promulgate ذيع 4

Prone, to be جثم

Proof بُرْهان to put to the p.
بلو 8

Prop أُثْفِيّة

Propagation كثر inf. 4

Property مال : أملاك .pl مُلْك
أَمْوال .pl

Prophet نَبِيّ

Proportion as, in كُلَّمَا in p. to
لِحَسَب

Propose عَرَض على i

Proprietor مالك, صاحِب

Prose نَثْر

Prosperity فَلاح

Prostrate oneself سجد u

Protect حمى i

Protection جِوار to receive p.
جور 3 : to give p. 4 : to demand
p. 10 : more protecting, elat.

Prove بلا (بلو) u inf. بَلاء to
cause to be proved 4

Proverb مَثَل pl. أمثال

Provide رزق u

Providence عِناية

Province لِواء, متصرّفيّة

Provisions, to take زود 5

Public عُمُومِيّ to make p. جَهَر a
in p. جهارًا

Publish نشر i, a

Pull جرّ u p. down هَدَمَ i p. off,
out نزع i p. up (horse) كبح a

Pulpit مِنْبَر

Punish عذب 2 p. in return
عقب 3

Punishment عقاب, عَذاب legal
p. حَدّ

Pure صحيح, (of blood) نَقِيّ
زكِيّ (soul) : عريق, أصيل
(water) صفو pc.

Purely مَحْض (adj.)

Purify زكو 5 : to p. oneself طهر 2

Purport مَآب

Purpose غَرَض

Purpose, to نوى i (a thing)
وخى 5

Purposely قَصْدًا

Push دَفَع a inf. دَفْع

Put جَعَل, وَضْع a inf. وضع a
p. off (postpone) tr. اخر 2,
intr. 5 : p. off (shoes) خلع a
p. on لَبِس a

Quake زلزل 2: to make to q. 1

Qualify كيف 2

Quality صفة pl. reg., good q. جُودة

Quantity كَمّيّة in large q. = with muchness

Quarrel مرى 6: to q. with 3

Quarrelsomeness شَراسة

Quarter (5½ bushels) إِردَبّ

Quarter one on أوّب 2: to take up one's quarters 5

Queen مَلكة

Quench the thirst of روى 4

Question مَسْألة pl. أسئلة (opp. to answer) سؤال

Quickly = in haste

Quiescence = *sukūn*

Quote قبس 8

Race (lineage) قَوْم, جِنْس, أُمّة pl. أجناس

Racial جنسى

Raciality جنسية

Rage غَيْظ to fall into a r. 5

Raid غَزْوة pl. reg.

Railway سكة حديديّة, سكّة, سَكة حديد

Rain مَطَر pl. أمطار

Rain on, to غيث i

Raise up رَفَع a

Raja رجاء

Rally كرّ u

Ramadan = Ramadānu

Rancour حقْد to harbour r. حَقَد i rancorous حَقُود

Rank (degree) رُتْبة to take r. صَفّ 8

Ransack بعثر

Ransom فَدَى i r. oneself 8

Rapier حُسام

Rare, to be ندر u

Rarely قَلّما

Rarity ندر pc. fem.

Al-Rashid الرشيد

Rashly, to deal خرق u

Rather than دون r. than that الأخْرَى the r. مِمّا or r. او بالاحرى

Raven غُراب

Raw (material) أوّلى

Razor مُوسَى

Reach مَدّى to come within reach of نوش 3: to be within r. of one another 6

Reach بَلَغَ u to r. out (the hand) to نول 6

Read قرأ a reader, pc. pl. قُرّاء

Ready to act, to be حفز 5 to make oneself r. أهب 5

Reality حقيقة in r. فى حقيقة أمْرِه

Realize حقّ 2

Really حقيقةً

Reap حَصَدَ u inf. حَصْد

Reapinghook مِنْجَل

Reason (cause) سبب by r. of بعامل, لسبب فى

Reassert = back

Rebel ثور u

Rebellion ثَوْرة

Receipts, see revenue

Recent حديث recently, acc.

Recite (Koran) (تلو) تلا u (poetry) نشد 4

Reciter (of Koran) حفظ pc. pl. حُفّاظ (of poetry) نشد pc. 4

Reckon عدّ u

Reckoning حُسْبان

Recognise درك i عرف 3 رعى 4

Recollect oneself, to ذكر 5

Reconcile وفق 2

Recorder حدث pc. 2

Recount قصّ u

Recourse to, to have نوب 4

Recover فوق 4

Recur = occur time after time

Red حمر elat. to grow red 9

Redeem شفع

Redemption فدًى

Reduce to straits حصر

Redundant زيد pc.

Refectory مَطْعَم

Reference مُناسَبة

Refined لطيف

Reflect = regard

Reform, to صلح 4 Reform, re-formation, inf. pl. إصلاحات reformer, pc.

Refrain = abstain

Refuge, to take لجأ 8 to seek r. عوذ u to say 'I seek r. in God' 10

Refuse أبَى a

Regard عبر 8 : regarding, in r. to فى

Regime = order

Region = direction

Register ديوان

Rehearse, inf. سَرْد

Reign مُلْك

171

Rejoice فرح a

Relate (tell) ورد 4 it is related حُكِىَ to r. oneself to نمى 8

Relation نِسْبة , عَلاقة pl. reg.

Relationship قُرْبة near r. قَرابة

Relatives أُسْرة

Relenting صَفْح

Relic أَثَر pl. آثار

Religion دين pl. أديان professor of r. 5 pc.

Religious دينى

Relinquish خلو عن 5

Reluctance رَغْم

Rely وكل 5

Remain بَقِىَ a to make r. 4

Remainder بَقِيّة

Remark, to = say

Remarkable نبغ , نبيه pc.

Remember ذَكَرَ u (by heart) حفظ a

Remind ذكر 4

Remonstrate عتب 3 remonstrance, inf. عتاب

Remorse نَدَم to feel r. ندم a

Remote بعيد pc. شسع to be r. بعد 8

Remove نزح a tr. بدّ 2 بعد 4

Renaissance = Rising

Render جعل a ردّ u

René-Taillandier رينه تياندييه

Renew جدّ 2

Renounce رفض i

Renown شأن

Rent, to be فطر 5

Reorganization = organization

Repair مَصْلَحة

Repair, to صلح 4 : repair, inf.

Repeat (do again) عود u (a thing) 4

Repel درأ a to r. mutually 6

Repent توب u

Repentance تَوْبة

Repentant تَوّاب

Repenting نَدامة

Replace رجع 4

Reply جوب 4

Report قرّ inf. 2

Represent مثل 2 (politically) نوب عن u representation, inf. نيابة

Repressing كَظْم

Republic جُمْهوريّة

Repulse ردّ u

Require حوج 8 with إلى : have no escape from

Requirement مَأْرَب

Requisite, to be قضى 8

Requisition, to حضر 10

Requital ثَواب

Requite ثوب 2 and 4

Rescue نقذ 4

Resemblance مَثَل

Resemble شبه 3 and 8 : 5 with ب

Resent سوء 8

Residence قوم inf. 4

Resident نزيل

Resist قوم 3

Resolution عزيمة, عَزْم

Resolve عَزَم i

Resort, to أوى i

Resources ثَرْوة

Respect (way) وَجْه pl. وُجُوه
(reverence) حرم inf. 8: in r.
of فى

Responsible كلف pc. pass. 2 :
to be r. for = to secure (debt)

Rest (remainder) سائر (peace)
راحة

Rest, to (of building) ركز 8
(repose) روح 10

Restful روح elat.

Resting-place مَرْقَد

Restore (give back) عود 4

Restrain كفّ u

Restrict قصر 8

Result, to حصل u inf. حُصُول
make to r. 2: result, pc.,
نتيجة

Resurrection قيامة

Resuscitate = make live

Retrace one's steps أثر 5

Retreat رَجْعة

Retreat, to رجع i

Return عَوْدة return journey
إياب

Return, to, intr. رجع i عود u :
tr. رّد رَجَع u : to r. (from
journey) قدم a : to r. to (the
attack) عود 3 : to make to r.
4 : to seek to return to 10

Reveal جلو 2 : to r. oneself 5
to be revealed 8 : (a secret)
ذيع 4

Revel ريفل

Revelation وَحْى to grant a r.
وحى 4

Revenge نقم inf. 8

Revenue ورد inf. 4, pl. fem. reg.

Revere حرم 8

Reverence, to وقى 8

Reverse عَكْس

Review فقد 5

Revile سبّ *u*

Revive نعش 8 :intr. 4 عود

Revolution (political) ثَوْرة

Revolve دور *u* tr. 2

Reward جَزاء

Reward جزَى *i* and 3

Rhyming consonant رَوِيّ

Ribbon شريطة

Rich غَنِيّ pl. أغنياء to think oneself r. 10

Riches غِنًى

Ride رَكَبَ *a* rider, pc.: inf. رُكوب r. behind رِدف 3

Right حَقّ, صواب pl. حُقوق

Right hand يمين pl. أيْمان

Rip up بقر *a*

Rise قوم *u* رقى 8: to begin to r. (star) بزغ

Rising نَهْضة

Rite مَعْشَر

River نَهْر pl. أنْهار

Road نَهْج, طُرُق pl. طرقات main road مَسْلَك

Rob, to, inff. سَرَق, سَلُب, سَرِقة

Robe ثَوْب pl. أثواب

Rock صَخْر pl. صُخور

Rôle of, to play the سلك مَسْلَك *u*

Roll, to دحرج

Roller مَنْدَرونة

Roof سَقْف

Room غُرْفة

Root أصْل to take r. 5: to r. out 10

Rope حَبْل

Rose وَرْد

Rough غليظ to rough it وحش 5

Roughly with, to deal غَلُظَ على

Round حَوْل

Rousseau, Jean Jacques جان جاك روسو

Rout هزم *i* pass. 7

Route طريق

Rub عرك *u* inf. عَرْك r. oneself حكّ 8

Ruddy = red

Rude جاهلى

Rude to, to be (جفو) جفا *u*

Rugged وَعْر

Ruin (moral) خَراب تَلَف

Ruin, to خرب 4

Rule, to سود *u*

Ruler (to draw lines) مِسْطَرة

Run جرى i (flow) رِكُض u
inf. جَرْى r. away (slave)
أَبَقَ u, i
Rush (upon) هجم i to r. blindly
in قحم 8
Russia الروسيا
Russian روسى

Saadat سادات
Sack زكيبة
Sacred قدس pc. pass. 2
Sacrifice ذبح a
Sadden حزن 4
Saddle رَحْل
Sadly = with grief
Safa, the = al-Ṣafā
Safe أَمن pc. سليم to be s. أمن
a to make s. 4: safer سلم elat.
Safely سلم pc. acc.
Safety خَلاص
Sagacious ذكى pl. أَذْكِياء
Sagacity ذَكاء
Sage = wise
Sailor ملّاح
Saint (St.) سان
Sake وَجْه, أَجْل
Saladin = the soundness of the Religion

Salih صالح
Salim سليم
Salisbury سالسبورى
Saloon صالون, قاعة
Salt مالِح adj. مُلْح
As-Salt السلط
Salute سلم على 2
Salvation سَلامة
Sandal نَعْل
Sanhedrin = sitting
Sardinia سردينيا
Satan, the = al-Shaitānu, pl. شياطين
Satiated, to be شبِع a
Satisfaction مَرْضاة
Satisfied, to be رضِى a to satisfy 4
Savage وَحْشىّ
Save = except : save that سِوَى أن
Save, to خلص 2
Say قول u sayer, pc.
Saying قَوْل
Scabbard غمد pl. غُمُود
Scarcely = not almost or almost not
Scare خوف 2: to be scared نفر u
Scatter بذر u inf. بَذْر
Scene, to come on the بَرَز u

Sceptical, to be ريب 8, Sceptic, pc.

Sceptre صَوْلَجان

School مَدْرَسة

Science عِلْم pl. عُلُوم

Scientific علمى

Scoff at سَخِرَ مِن a

Scour سَيْل pl. سُيول

Scrape بَحَثَ a inf. بَحْث

Scream صَخِبَ a

Script خَطّ

Scrub شُجَيْر

Scruple رَهْبة

Sea بَحْر pl. بحار

Search فتش inf. 2

Season (of year) فَصْل

Seat مَقْعَد (centre) مقام

Seclude oneself خلو 8 seclusion, inf. 5

Second ثانٍ adv. acc.

Secret سِرّ

Secret, adj. سِرّى

Secret, to tell as, keep s., tell secretly سرّ 4

Sect = way

Section = piece : (people) فريق

Secure (debt) كفل u

Security (safety) أَمْن, أمان (pledge) ضَمانة

Sedative سكن pc. 2 fem.

Sedition فِتْنة

Seduce غرّ u

See, see good رأى a

Seed زَرْع

Seeing that إِذْ

Seek لمس 8 طَلَبَ u

Seeking طَلَب

Seem ظهر a

Seize أَخَذَ u inf. أَخْذ

Select جبى 8

Selection نقى inf. 8

Self نَفْس, ذات pl. أَنْفُس

Selfish ذاتى

Sell بيع i seller, pc. pl. باعة

Semi- شِبْه

Send بَعَثَ a وسل 4: s. down نزل 4: s. up صدر 4

Sending رسالة

Sensible of, to be حسّ ب 4

Sentence قَضاء

Sentiment = opinion : (feeling) عاطفة

Separate فصل i pass. 7

Series سِلْسِلة

Serious = important

Seriousness = importance

Serpent حَيّة

Serve خدم u servant, pc., pl.
خَدَم (of God) عبد pl. عباد
service خِدْمة to take into s.
10

Set (sun) غرب u inf. غُرُوب: (star)
أفل u: s. about a thing قومب
جهرب u: s. before oneself (aim)
3: s. forth (expound) فصح 4:
s. out رحل 8: to be set (to
tune) طبق على 7

Settled, to be قرّ 10

Settled country حَضارة

Seven سبع

Seventh سابع

Seventy سبعون

Shade (spoil) فَيْء

Shadow ظلّ

Shake هزّ u

Shame فضيحة

Shame, to be put to خَزِيَ a to
put to s. 4

Shape هَيْأة

Share نصيب

Shave حلق i and 2

Shed سفك i inf. سَفْك

Sheikh شيخ pl. مشايخ, (chiefs)
شُيوخ

Shelter oneself أوى i shelter
8 لجأ to find s. مَأْوًى

Sherif شريف

Sherifian شريفى

Shield, to become a جنّ

Shine (زهو) زها u

Ship سفينة pl. سُفُن coll. سفين

Shoaib = Shu'aibun

Shock دَهْشة

Shoe = sandal

Shoe (oneself) حذا (حذو) u
inf. حَذْو

Shoot = beat

Shoot out دلع 7

Shop حانوت, دُكّان

Shore شاطئ

Short قصير to be s. قَصَرَ u to
fall s. 2: to shorten oneself 6

Shortly after = after by a little

Shoulder كَتِف

Shout صرخ 8

Show رأى 4 ظهر 4

Shrink قلص i

Shrivel شمأز 4

Shrub شُجَيْرة pl. reg.

Shun عرض عن 4

Siberia سبيريا Siberian سبيري

Sick مريض to be s. مَرِض a
sickness مَرْضة

Side جَنْب (also abstr.) جَنْب
(of a compartment) شِقّ (party)
طائفة

Siege حصار

Siffin صفّين

Sigh حَسْرة pl. حَسَرات

Sighing زَفير

Sight بَصَر pl. أبصار to sight 4

Sign آية

Signet-ring خاتَم

Significance = importance

Signify عرف 2

Silence سُكُوت

Silent سكت pc. to silence 4

Silt طَمَّى

Silver فِضّة

Similar to على مِثال

Similarly = like that

Simplicity بَساطة

Sin إثْم

Sin, to, inf. خَطَأ

Sinai = Sīnīnu, Saina'u

Since مُنْذُ, حَيْثُ, إِذْ

Sincere كريم, حقيقى

Sing (recite) نشد 4

Singing غِناء

Single فرد pc. pass. 4: to be s. 7:
singleness, inf. 4: single (after
neg.) مِن

Sink غرق 4

Sit جَلَس i inf. جُلُوس s. with 3

Sitting مَجْلِس

Six سِتّ

Sixty ستون

Skilful نِطاسىّ

Skill نَبالة

Skirt ذَيْل pl. أذيال

Sky سَماء

Slab لَوْح, لوحة

Slaughter مذبح

Slaughter, to ذَبَح a and 2

Slave عَبْد pl. عَبيد slavegirl
جارية

Slay قَتَل u slain قتيل

Sleep مَنام

Sleep, to نوم a inf. نَوْم

Sleepingplace مضجع

Slender نحيف elat. هيف

Slightness هَوان

Slip هَفْوة

178

Slip, to زلّ i

Sloping حدر inf. 7, pl. fem.

Slow بطىء

Slumber وَسِنَ a inf. سِنَة

Small صَغير to think s. 10:
حقير (poor) (of number)=few

Small-pox جَدَرِيّ

Smile بسم 5

Smoke دُخان

Smooth, to مهد 2: to become s.
5: smoothest, elat.

Snatch خطف a

Sneeze عطس i

Snow ثَلْج snowy ثلجى

So كَذَا وكَذَا so and so ف so
far بحَيْث so that حَتَّى الآن
and so on إلى غير ذلك

Soap صابون

Soar حلق 2

Social اجتماعى

Society جمع pc. pass. 8 (association, committee) جَمْعِيّة

Soft لَيِّن deal softly with 3:
رُخاء (wind)

Softness لين

Soil = earth

Soldier جنود pl. جُنْد coll. جندى

Solemnize حفل ب 8

Solid مَتين

Solidarity عَصَبِيّة

Sollicitous about, to be عنى ب 8

Sollicitude همّ inf. 8

Solomon = Sulaymānu

Some بعض some...other...
من بعض some of

Sometimes = now and then: قد
with impf.

Son ابْن pl. بَنون reg.

Soon للحال: = when a short time
had passed away: as s. as
كُلَّما

Soporific نعس pc. 4 fem.

Sorrow حُزْن

Sorrowing رقيق

Sorry, to be رقّ i

Sort نَوْع pl. أنواع in some s.
نوعًا ما

Soudanese سودانى

Soul نَفْس pl. نُفوس ,أنْفُس
نَسَمَة (person)

Sound صَوْت

Sound, to be صَلُحَ u sound,
adj. = pc.: (opinion) جَزيل,
سَديد

Soundness صَلاح

South جنوب southwards, acc.

Southern جنوبي

Sovereignty رئاسة

Sow, to زرع inf. زَرْع sowings, pc. pass. fem. pl.

Space ظَرْف (of time) مُدّة

Spade مِحْفَر

Sparing, to be قصد 8

Spark شرارة

Speak to كلّم 2: to s.(mutually) 5

Special خصّ pc., خُصوصي

Specify عين 2

Spectacle مَنْظَر

Speech خُطْبة, لَهْجة, قَوْل, كَلام

Speedy وشيك

Spell on, to cast a سخر 2

Spend (money) نفق 4: (time) قضى i

Spendthrift, to be سرف 4

Sphere = circle

Spirit (opp. of letter) = meaning: (soul) رُوح pl. أَرْواح

Spiritual = religious

Spite فعل inf. 7

Spite of, in رَغْمًا عن

Splendid فخر pc.

Split, to شقّ u, pass. 7

Spoil, to نهب a inf. نَهْب

Spot موقع

Spread شيع i inf. شُيُوع s. abroad نشر u

Spring عَيْن fem., pl. عُيُون

Spring, adj. ربيعي

Spring up (grow) نشأ a

Spurious كذب pc.

Spy, to جسّ 5 لَمَح a to s. out

Squander تلف 4

Square, to ربع 2

Stable إصْطُبْل

Stake خطر 3

Stamboul = Constantinople

Stamp (feet) خبط 5 : s. on, 2 : (cloth) علم 4

Stamping خَبْط

Stand, intr. قوم u inf. قِيام, tr. وقف i to s. by = to s. upon the side of: to s. to receive orders, inf. مُثول to s. still وقف i inf. وُقُوف to come to a standstill, 5

Standard مِقْياس, قِياس adj. صاغ

Star نَجْم pl. نُجُوم

Start (a work) أخذ في u

Starvation سَغْب

State (country) ولاية pl. reg. (condition) حال fem., pl. حالة s. of things أَحْوال

Statement قَوْل

Statesman = politician

Station (railway) مَحَطّة pl. reg.
(rank) مَنْزِلة

Statistics إحصاءات

Stay قوم 4

Steal سَرَق i

Steam, adj. بُخارى

Steamship باخِرة

Step in دخل 6

Steppes فيافٍ pl.

Stiff climb عَقَبَة pl. reg.

Stifle خنق u أخذ بخِناق

Still, to هدأ 2

Stint, to قتر عن u

Stipulate عهد الى

Stir up (dust) ثور 4

Stocks فَلَقَة

Stoker وقّاد

Stone حَجَر (of a ring) فَصّ

Stone, adj. حجرى

Stop (train) وقف i tr. 2 : stop
up (well) inf. رَدْم

Store, to خزن u inf. خَزْن

Store up for oneself ذخر 8

Storehouse عَنْبَر

Storm = violent (wind), pl.
عواصف

Story حِكاية

Straight قَويم

Strained (compulsory) إجْبارى

Strained, to be وتر 5

Strange غَريب

Straw قَشّ chopped s. تِبْن

Stray (from faith) مَرق inf.
مُروق

Stream نَهْر

Street شارِع

Strength قُوّة pl. قُوَى

Strengthen (of : 2 قوى 2 أيد
plant) أزر 3

Stress ضَرّ

Stretch out بَسَط u, مَدّ u to s.
the neck شرأب 4

Strict حفظ pc. 3

Strictly orthodox على المذهب
الأَضْيَق

Strife خِصام

Strike = hit

Striking منظرى

String, to نظم i

Strive خصم 6 and 8 : to s. with 3

Strong قَوِىّ to be s. قوى a

Struggle عِراك

Struggle, to نفس 6

Student طَلَب pc. pl. طُلَّاب, طَلَبَة

Study دَرْس, دِراسة

Study, to درس u to s. together 6

Stuff (cloth) قُماش

Stumble عَثْرة

Stumble, to عثر u, i

Stupid = fool

Subaltern رأْس pc. pass.

Subdue ولى 10

Subject (of discourse) مَبْحَث, وضع pc. pass.

Subjects رَعِيّة pl. رعايا

Submission خُضُوع, رضوخ

Submit خضع a

Subside نقص u

Subsisting قَيُّوم

Substance (of discourse) خُلاصة

Substitute نائب

Succeed (follow) تلا (تلو) u نَجَح (not fail) u خلف a to s. to وَلِيَ i

Success نَجاح

Successor خَليفة to make s. خلف 2

Succour, to ask for عون 10

Such = like that, etc.: such as = as, like: such a one فُلان

Suckle رضع 4

Suckling رَضيع

Sudden فَجائِى

Suddenly بَغْتَةً

Suet, a bit of شَحْمة

Suffice كفى i to s. one against, c. d. a.: to s. oneself 8

Sufficiency حَسْب

Sufficient كفى pc. or impf. with acc.

Sufi صوفى pl. صوفيّة

Suit وفق i

Suitable, to be أتى 5

Sukūn سكون

Suleiman the Magnificent سليمان القانونجى

Sully لطخ a

Sultan سلطان sultanic سلطانى

Sum جُمْلة

Summary لخص pc. pass. 2

Summit قِمّة pl. قِمَم

Summon (دعو) دعا u to be summoned (jury) ندب 8

Summons دَعْوة

Sun شَمْس

Sundry نوع pc. 5

Supererogatory thing نافلة

Superior فضل elat.

Supplicate ضرع 5

Supplication دُعاء

Supply مدّ 4

Support مُساعدة

Supposable حمل pc. pass. 8

Suppress كتم u

Sure of, to make يقن ب 4

Surety ضمن pc.

Surface سَطْح

Surpass زيد عن i

Surpassing فوق pc.

Surround حوط 4 with acc.
or ب

Survey طلع 8

Surviving = in the bond of life

Suspect وهم, خَشِيَ a, 8

Suspend عطل 2

Swallow بلع a

Sway = strength

Swear الو 4

Sweep كَنْس inf.

Sweetmeat فالوذ

Swerve عَنَدَ u

Swift سريع

Swim عَوْم u inf. عَوْم

Swoop قَصّ 7

Sword سَيْف pl. سُيُوف

Syed سَيّد

Sympathetic ولى pc. 3

Sympathise = feel along with

Sympathy = inclination

Syria الشَّأْم

Syrian سُورىّ

System نِظام pl. fem. reg.

Table مائدة

Tabuk تبوك

Tact حوط inf. 8

Take أَخذ u t. to oneself 8: to t.
to الى i t. place وقع a t.
self off from عزل 8: t. in turns
نوب 6

Tale قِصّة pl. قِصَص

Talib طالب

Talk كَلام, حَديث

Talk to, to حدث 3: to t. together 6

Tall طويل

Tangier طَنْجة

Tank صِهْريج

Tap (of drum) قَرع

Tarry مكث a لَبَث u

Task هَمّ pc. 4 fem.

Task, to كلف 2

Taste, to ذوق u to make to t. 4

Tavern حانة pl. reg.

Tax جباية

Teach علمِ 2, teacher, pc.

Teaching = doctrines

Tear دمعة pl. دُموع

Telegram تلغراف pl. fem. reg.

Telegraphic = lightning

Tell قول u

Temporal=worldly or=transient

Temptation بَلْوَى

Ten عشر

Tenacious = violent

Tendency = inclination

Tender شفيق

Tent خَيْمة pl. خيام

Tent-pole عِماد pl. عَمَد

Term (of life) أجَل

Terrible هول pc.

Terrify ذعر a

Terror هَوْل pl. أهْوال

Test محن a, pass. 8

Tether عقال

Tewfik وفق inf. 2

Thamud = Thamūdu

Than مِنْ

Thank شكر u

Thanks شُكُور pl.

That, conj. أنْ, أنَّ in order that كَىْ, لِ, لكى

That, pron. ذَلكَ &c.

Then عند ذلك, ثُمَّ, فَ

Theocratic إلَهِى

There, there is, are هُنَاك

Thereafter ثُمَّ

Therefore = for that

These هَؤُلَاءِ

Thick كثيف, سميك

Thickness سَمْك

Thief لصّ pl. لُصُوص

Thigh فَخِذ

Thing شَيْء pl. أشياء

Think ظنّ u (imagine) 5: وهم to t. twice أمل 5

Thinking ظَنّ, فكُر

Third ثالث thirdly, acc. ثُلُث $\frac{1}{3}$

Thirst ظِمْء t. for revenge غَليل

Thirst, to ظمئ a inf. ظَمَأ

Thirsting عَطَش

Thirsty عَطْشَان

Thirty ثَلَاثون

This هَذَا &c.

Thistles شَوْك

Thorn قَتَاد

Those أُولَائكَ

Thought (abstract) فِكْر, خَاطِر
pl. فكريّة أفكار.

Thousand أَلْف pl. أُلُوف

Thread خَيْط

Threat وعيد

Threaten هدّ 2, threatening, inf.

Three ثَلاث

Thresh دوس u

Threshing-floor بَيْدَر

Throne عَرْش, كُرْسِيّ

Through ب

Throw, throw away, down رَمَى i
lit. to pelt: to t. off نزع i inf.
رفع to t. up, inf. نَزْع

Thrust دعّ u

Thunder رَعْد

Thus هٰكَذا

Thwart عرض 3

Tiding, good بشيرة to bring g. t.
بشر 2: to tell g. t. mutually 6

Tie رابطة

Tie, to رَبَطَ i, pass. 8

Tieling لنغ تاى

Tigris, the دِجْلة

Time مَرّة, زَمَن (long) زَمَن, pl.
أَوْقَات pl. وَقْت, (of prayer)reg.,
t. after t. حين بَعْد حينا at
one t. ذاتَ يَوْمِ, فى زمن معيّن

at the same t. فى الوقت نفسه,
(upon that): at على أن adv.
that t. حينئذٍ in the t. of
the times على عَهْد الدَّهْر

Timely, to be حين i

Times, the (newspaper) التيمس

Tinsel زخرفة

Tired, to be عيّ 4

Title عُنْوان

To ل, إلى

Together مَعًا

Tomb مَقْبُرة

Tongue لسان pl. أَلْسِنة

Tooth ناب

Torch سِراج

Totter دعو 6

Touch مسّ a

Towards إلى, (of place) نَحْو, (of
time) فى

Tower (up), to شمخ

Town بَلَد, بَلْدة or = city

Trace أَثَر pl. آثار.

Track, to (قفو) قفا u

Traffic تجارة adj. تجاريّ

Traffic, to تجر 3

Train (camels, railway) قطار
masc., pl. قطارات

Train, to (rear) ربو 2 درس 2

Traitor غدر pc. : to be t. خون u

Trample down = tread

Transfer حول 2

Transgress عدو 5 : to t. (against) 8, transgression, inf.

Transient, to be فني i

Transport, to نَقَل u inf. نَقْل to t. oneself 8

Trap رَصَد

Travel سير i inf. سَيْر, مَسِير to t. by night سرى 4

Treacherous = traitor

Treachery غَدْر pl. غَدَرات

Tread وَطْأَة

Tread, to وطئ a to t. down درس u to t. out (corn) دوس u

Treasure ذخيرة

Treasury خزانة pl. reg.

Treat علج 3, (things) عمل 3

Treatment مُعَامَلة, (medical) علاج

Treaty with, to make عهد 3 treaty, inf. معاهدة

Tree شَجَرَة pl. أَشْجار

Treeshaped شجر pc. pass. 2

Trench أُخْدُود

Trial مِحْنة, pl. مِحَن

Tribe قبيلة, حَىّ

Trick حيلة

Trifle, to عبث a

Trifling تفه pc.

Trim عمر 2

Triumph نصر inf. 8

Trouble ضرب, مشقّة pl. مشاقّ inf. 8

Troubled, to be ضرب 8

Troublesome شقّ pc.

Trough حَوْض

Truce هُدْنة

True صدق pc., (real) حقيقى to speak t. صَدَق u, to declare t. 2

Trumpet صُور

Trust وَصاية

Truth حَقّ, حقيقة in t. acc.

Truthful, truth speaking, to be, صَدَق u truthful, pc.

Try جرب 2 : (deceitfully) حول 3 : (endeavour) سعى a (test) بلو (بلو) u

Tumble سَقَطَ u inf. سُقُوط

Tunis تونس Tunisian تونسى

Turban عمامة

Turco-Egyptian = Egyptian Turk

Turk تُرْكى pl. أَتْراك

Turkey تركيّا

Turn دَوْرة, نَوْبة to take in turns نوب 6

Turn, to, tr. لفت *i*, intr. 8, ولى 2:
(mill) دور 4: t. aside, tr. جَنَح
a, intr. 8: t. away (from)
عرض 4: t. away in disgust
= loathe: t. back ردّ *u*, inf.
مَرَدّ, رَدّ t. one's back دبر 4:
t. (fleeing) ولى 2: t. round
قلب 7: t. towards أمّ *u*

Tus طوس

Twelve اثنا عشر

Twenty, Twentieth عشرون

Twine, to بوم 4

Two اثْنان

Type مثال, طِراز

Tyrannicide = killing of tyrant

Tyrant جَبّار

Uff, Uff, to say أقّ 5

Ugly قبيح

Umaiyah أمَيّة

Unadulterated مَحْض

Uncle عَمّ

Uncover كشف *i*

Under تَحْت

Understand فَهِم *a* عَقَل *i*

Understanding فَهْم

Undertaking شرع pc. pass.

Unfortunately = for the evil of
the fortune

Unhappy, to be حَزِن *a* to make
unh. حَزَن *u*

Uniform طَقْم

Union جمع inf. 8, place of u.
مَجْمَع

Unique وحيد

Unite جمع *a*, (form an
opinion) بَيّن 8

Unity وَحْدة

Universal عُمُومى

Universalize طلق 4

Unknown نكر pc. pass. 4

Unlawful حَرام to pronounce,
declare unl. حرم 2

Unloose حَلّ *u*

Unpremeditated بديهىّ

Unsheath خرط 8

Untie فكّ *u*

Until حَتّى u. that إلى أن

Unto إلى

Up, upon عَلَى

Upper علو elat.

Uproar صَخَب

Upside down, to be قلب *a*, u. d.
= pc. pass.

Use عمل 10

Useful نفع pc.

Usually على الغالب, غالبا

Utmost غاية

Vacate خلو 4

Vain بطل pc., to render v. 4

Valley وادٍ pl. أوْدية, ودْيان open v. بقاع pl.

Valuable ثمين

Value (price) ثَمَن, قيمة, (worth) قَدر

Value, to قدر i, u

Vary خلف 8, various, pc.

Vatican, the الفاتيكان

Vault حَنيّة

Vault (a building), to قبو 4

Vegetables بَقْل

Veil, to سَتَرَ u, to v. oneself 8

Vein عرق pl. عروق

Venal شوه pc. pass. 2

Venerable جليل, مَهيب

Veneration هَيْبة

Vengeance ثأر

Venice بُنْدُقيّة

Venture قدم 4, venturesome-ness, inf.

Veracity صِدق

Verify حقّ 2, verification, inf.

Verily إنَّ

Verse (of Koran) آيَة (of poem) بَيْت pl. أبيات

Very جدّ acc.

Vestibule إيوان

Vestige رَسْم

Veto, to نَهى نهى inf.

Vexation جَزَع

Vibration رج inf. 8

Viceroy عمل pc.

Vicissitude تَقَلُّبات

Victoria فيكتوريا

Victorious over, to be ظفِر ب a victor, pc.

View منظر, مرأى

Views = opinions

Village قَرْية pl. قُرًى

Vines عنَب

Violence شِدّة

Violent شديد to act violently, 4: to become v. 8: v. (of wind) عصف pc.

Virility مَتانة

Virtue فضيلة

Visible, to be بدا (بدو) u, to make v. 4

Vision رُؤْية

Visit زور u, (sick) عود u

Visitation زيارة

Visitor زور pc. pl. زوّار

Voice صَوْت

Void, to be حَبِطَ a

Volcano بُرْكان

Vowel = motion

Wade خوض u

Wa-fang-tien وا فانج تين

Wage holy war جهد 3, inf. جهاد

Wait نظر 8 Wait! = have patience

Wake up, to نبه 8, يقظ 5

Waking يَقَظَة

Wali, to become وَلِيَ i Wali, pc., pl. ولاية Waliship وُلاة

Walk مَشَى i

Wall (of جِدار, جَدْر pl. جُدْران town) سُور pl. أسوار

Want (lack) عَدَم

Want (wish) بغى i, (lack) رود 4 عدم a to w. for oneself بغى 8

War حَرْب fem., pl. حُرُوب Holy war جهاد

War, adj. حربى

War with, to حرب 3 : to w. mutually 6

Ward صون u : w. off, inf. دَفْع to seek to w. off from each other 6

Ware of, to be حَذِرَ a inf. حِذْر to bid beware 2

Wares بضائع pl.

Warm دفئ

Warn نذر 4

Warner نَذير

Al-Warraq الوَرّاق

Wash غسل i inf. غَسْل

Washington واشنطون

Wasif وصيف

Waste = dissipate : to become wasted away بَلِيَ a

Watch رقب 3 : w. (for) 8 : keep w. over حرس u inf. حِراسة watchman, pc.

Water ماء pl. مياه

Watering place مَنْهَل, مَوْرِد

Wave موج pl. أمْواج

Wave, to لوح 2

Waxcloth شمع pc. pass. 2

Way طَريقة, طَريق pl. طُرُق the ways of the winds أَدْراج الرّياح

Wazeer وزير

Weak ضَعيف

Weak, to be ضَعُف to make w. 4 : to think w. 10

Weakness ضُعْف

Weak points أَوْجُه الضَّعف (respects of weakness)

Weal سَلامة

Wealth ثَرْوة

Wealthy = rich

Wear لَبِسَ a w. out نهك 8

Weariness تَعَب

Weather جَوّ

Wedding عُرْس

Week أُسْبُوع Weekly أسبوعىّ

Weep بَكَى i make w. 4

Weigh كيل i

Weight مِثْقال

Welcome to مَرْحَبًا ب

Welfare عافية

Well بِئْر fem., pl. آبار

Well, adv. جَيِّدًا : cognate inf.

Well, to do = to do good

Were it not for لولا

West غَرْب westwards, acc.

Western غربىّ w. part مَغْرِب

What ما, أَىّ whatever مَهْمَا

Wheat قَمْح

Wheel round حول 5

When إذا, لَمّا When? مَتَى (at the time) when حِين

Whence = from where

Whenever إذا ما

Where? أَيْنَ where حَيْثُ

Whether...or أَ...أَمْ

Which أَىّ

While, for a = a space from the time

Whilst حِينما, بينما, بَيْنَا

Whisper وسوس

White بيض elat. to become w. 9

Who, whoever, he who مَنْ, اَلَّذى

Whole كُلّ, جَميع

Whole, to be سَلِمَ a

Wicked فجر pc.

Wide, to be رَحُبَ u

Wife زَوْجة

Wilderness صَحْراء pl. صَحارَى

Wilds بَرِّيّة

Will, to شيأ a

Win كسب i

Wind ريح fem.

Window نافذة

Wine خَمْر, خمرة pl. خمور

Wink at غضى عن 4

Winnow ذرى

Winter شتاء adj. شَتَوِيّ

Wisdom حِكْمَة

Wise حَكيم pl. حُكَماء

Wish, to رود 4

Wisp ضغث pl. أَضْغاث

With ب, (along with) مَعَ, فى, (before) عِنْد, لَدَى

Wither محل 4

Withhold ردع a

Within داخِل

Without مِن غير, (before inf.) بدون w. that من دون ان

Witness شهيد pl. شهود false w. شاهد الزُور

Witness, to شهد 3

Wizened ذبل pc.

Woe وَيْل, ويلة pl. reg., woe is me وَيْلَك woe be to you ويلتى

Woman اِمْرَأَة with art. المَرْأَة pl. نساء

Womankind أُنْثَى

Wonder عَجَب and no w. ولا غَرْو

Wonder, to عَجِب a with من to w. to oneself 5

Wonderful عجيب

Wont دأب

Wood خَشَب, piece of w. خشبة (forest) غابة pl. reg.

Wood, wooden = of wood

Word كَلِمة pl. reg.

Wording كِلَم

Work عَمَل pl. أَعْمال

Work, to عَمِلَ a to w. for (an object) عمل عَلَى to w. (a machine) شغل 8

Working عَمَل

World عالَم pl. reg.: this w. الدُّنْيَا

Worldly دنيوى

Worm دُودة

Wormwood شيح

Worse, worst شَرّ

Worship, to عَبَدَ u inf. عبادة

Worshipper عبد pl. عباد

Worth خَليق ب

Worthy of أهل ل

Worthy, to be حقّ 10

Would that! لَيْتَ would that I ليتنى he would وَدّ a he would that لو a ودّ لو

Wrest حول 3

Wrestle with صرع 3, wrestler, pc.

Write كَتَبَ u writer, pc. pl. كُتَّاب w. officially رَسَمَ u

Writing كتابة

Wrong, to ظلم i inf. ظُلْم wrong-doer, wrong-doing, pc.: wronging greatly ظلّام

Wrought فعل

Yacht يخت ,مَرْكَب

Yahya يحيى

Yathrib = Yaṯhribu

Yazdayard يزديرد

Yazid يزيد

Year عامر ,سَنة pl. سِنون

Yearn نزع i yearning حَنين

Yell صرخ u

Yellow صفر elat.

Yen-tai ين تاى

Yes نَعَمْ

Yoke نير

You أنْتَ ,أنْتُمْ yours = to you

Young = small: still y. فى مقتبَل العُمْر

Youthful فتى fem. فَتاة

Zacharias = Zakarīyā'a (gen.)

Zaid زيد

Zaiyat زيّات

Zeal غَيْرة

Zealous غَيور

Al-Zubeir الزبير

Zuhair زهير

ERRATA

Page 115 *after* "Absent, to be غيب *i* inf." *add* مغيب

    ,,   118, line 14 *after* "pass." *add* comma

    ,,   119, line 13 *delete* ظهر *a*

    ,,   120 *after* "Assassinate" *add* comma

    ,,   124, line 10 *for* لَبِدة *read* لَبِنة

For EU product safety concerns, contact us at Calle de José Abascal, 56–1°, 28003 Madrid, Spain or eugpsr@cambridge.org.

www.ingramcontent.com/pod-product-compliance
Ingram Content Group UK Ltd.
Pitfield, Milton Keynes, MK11 3LW, UK
UKHW012328130625
459647UK00009B/130